PYTHON PRAGMATICS: A PRACTICAL APPROACH

Mastering Python

Dr. Sangeetha G
Associate Professor
Department of Computer Science
CHRIST University

Dr. Sabarmathi G
Assistant Professor
School of Business and Management
CHRIST University

Dr. Hanumanthappa M
Senior Professor
Department of Computer Science and Applications
Bangalore University

INDEX

UNIT 1 - INTRODUCTION TO PYTHON

1.1 Overview of Python

Python is a powerful, high-level, general-purpose programming language created by *Guido van Rossum* in 1991. It is widely known for its simplicity, readability, and flexibility. Python is used across multiple domains, including:

- **Web Development:** Frameworks like Django and Flask make it easy to build scalable web applications.
- **Data Science & Machine Learning:** Libraries like Pandas, NumPy, and TensorFlow help analyze data and build machine learning models.
- **Automation:** Python is often used to automate repetitive tasks, such as file handling and web scraping.
- **Game Development:** Libraries like Pygame allow developers to build 2D games.
- **Scripting:** Python is a popular choice for scripting and backend tasks, making it a favorite among system administrators.

1.2 Key Features of Python

1) **Easy to Learn:** Python's simple syntax and structure make it accessible for beginners, allowing for quick learning and productivity.
2) **Interpreter-Based:** Python code is executed line by line, making debugging easier and providing immediate feedback during development.
3) **Interactive:** Python supports interactive mode, enabling users to test code snippets and experiment in real-time.
4) **Multi-Paradigm:** Python supports multiple programming styles, including procedural, object-oriented, and functional programming, allowing flexibility in design.
5) **Large Standard Library:** Python comes with a comprehensive library of modules and functions that facilitate various tasks, reducing the need for external packages.
6) **Open-Source & Cross-Platform:** Being open-source allows free usage and distribution, while cross-platform compatibility ensures Python works on different operating systems.
7) **GUI Development:** Python supports various libraries for building graphical user interfaces, making it suitable for desktop applications.
8) **Database Connectivity:** Python offers libraries to connect with different databases, enabling data manipulation and storage for applications.
9) **Extensible:** Python can integrate with other languages like C and C++, allowing developers to enhance performance and reuse existing code.
10) **Strong Developer Community:** A large and active community contributes to extensive documentation, resources, and third-party libraries, fostering support and collaboration.

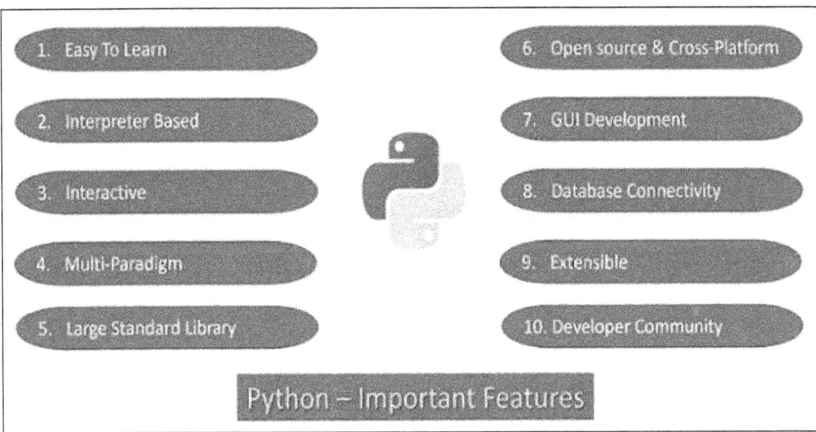

1.3 Limitations of Python

- Slower execution compared to compiled languages like C or Java.
- High memory usage, making it less efficient for memory-intensive tasks.
- Weak in mobile computing and app development.
- Not ideal for CPU-intensive tasks due to its interpreted nature.
- Global Interpreter Lock (GIL) restricts multithreading performance.
- Dependency on external libraries for some advanced features.
- Less suitable for low-level system programming.

1.4 Python IDE's

Python has evolved significantly since its inception, with each version introducing new features and improvements. Understanding the differences between major releases helps developers utilize the language more effectively and ensure compatibility in their projects. Here's a list of a few popular Python IDEs :

- PyCharm
- Visual Studio Code (VS Code)
- Spyder
- Atom
- Sublime Text
- IDLE
- Jupyter Notebook
- PyDev

1.5 Installing Python

To start coding in Python, you'll need to install Python and an Integrated Development Environment (IDE). Jupyter Notebook is one of the most popular IDEs, especially for data science and interactive coding.

Follow these steps to install Jupyter Notebook:

→ **Install Python:**
- Go to the official Python website.
- Download the latest Python version for your operating system.

- During installation, ensure the "Add Python to PATH" checkbox is selected.
- Install Jupyter Notebook:
- Open your terminal (or command prompt).
- Type the following command:
    # pip install notebook
- This command will install Jupyter Notebook on your machine.

→ **Launch Jupyter Notebook:**
- After installation, type the following in the terminal:
    # jupyter notebook

Jupyter Notebook will open in your browser, allowing you to create new notebooks and start writing Python code.

UNIT 2 - GETTING STARTED WITH PYTHON

2.1 Writing Your First Python Program

Let's start with a classic introduction to programming: the 'Hello, World!' program. This simple script will help you understand how to write and execute your first line of code in Python.

Step 1: Open Jupyter Notebook.

Step 2: Click on a new **code cell** to start typing.

Step 3: Type the following code:

```
print('Hello, World!')
```

Step 5: Run the code by pressing **Shift + Enter** or clicking the **Run** button.

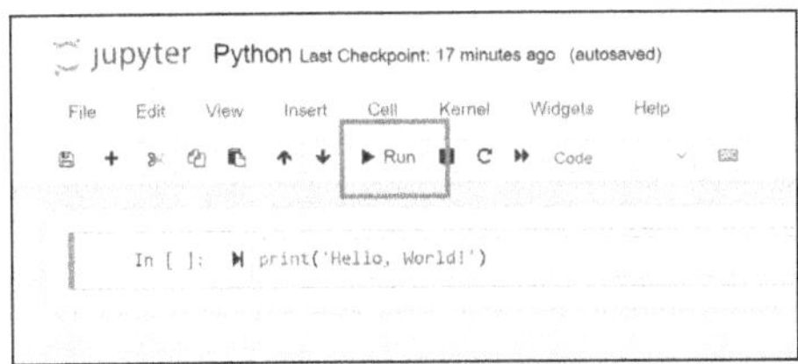

Step 6: Check the result below the cell, you should see **Hello, World!**

OUTPUT :

```
In [2]:  print('Hello, World!')
         Hello, World!
```

2.2 Python Data Types

Python, as a dynamically typed language, allows you to work with a variety of data types. These data types define how the interpreter will handle and store data during program execution. Some of the most commonly used data types in Python are Lists, Tuples, and Dictionaries. In this section, we'll explore these data types, how they work, and provide examples to demonstrate their use.

2.2.1 Lists in Python:

A list is a mutable, ordered sequence of elements in Python. Lists can store items of different data types (e.g., integers, strings, floats) and are defined using square brackets []. They support operations like indexing, slicing, and appending elements.

Example:

```
list1=['abcd', 345, 3.2,'python', 3.14]
list2=[234, 'xyz']
```

List Operations: Provided below is a list of common list operations, demonstrating how to access elements, slice lists, repeat, and concatenate them. These examples will help you understand how lists can be manipulated in various ways.

Code	Comment	Result
print list1	# prints complete list	['abcd', 345, 3.2,'python', 3.14]
print list1[0]	# prints first element of the list	abcd
print list1[-1]	#prints last element of the list	3.14
print list1[1:3]	# prints elements starting from index 1 to 2 # prints list1[start_at : end_at-1]	[345, 3.2]
print list1[2:]	#prints list starting at index 2 till end of the list	[3.2, 'python', 3.14]
print list 2 * 2	# asterisk (*) -is the repetition operator. Prints the list two times.	['abcd', 345, 3.2, 'python', 3.14, 234, 'xyz']
print list1 + list2	# prints concatenated lists	['abcd', 345, 3.2,'python', 3.14, 234, 'xyz']

Q: *Write a program to create two lists containing different data types and print their values.*

Step 1: Open Jupyter Notebook.

Step 2: Create a new file.

Step 3: Rename the file (e.g., **list_example.ipynb**).

Step 4: In a new code cell, type the following code to create two lists:

```
# list1 = ['abcd', 345, 3.2, 'python', 3.14]
# list2 = [234, 'xyz']
```

Step 5: Print the list using the print statement

```
# print(list1)
# print(list2)
```

Step 6: Run the code by pressing **Shift + Enter** or clicking the **Run** button.

Step 6: Check the result below the cell.

Output:

```
▶ list1 = ['abcd', 345, 3.2, 'python', 3.14]
  list2 = [234, 'xyz']

  print(list1)
  print(list2)

  ['abcd', 345, 3.2, 'python', 3.14]
  [234, 'xyz']
```

2.2.2 Tuples in Python:

A tuple is an immutable, ordered collection of items, typically used when the data should not be changed. Like lists, tuples can store different data types, but they are defined using parentheses ( ). Tuples are faster than lists due to their immutability.

Example:

> # tuple1= ('abcd', 345 , 3.2,'python', 3.14)
> # tuple2= (234, 'xyz')

Code	Comment	Result
print tuple1	# prints complete tuple1	('abcd', 345, 3.2, 'python', 3.14)
print tuple1[0]	# prints first element of the tuple1	abcd
print tuple1[-1]	#prints last element of the tuple1	3.14
print tuple1[1:3]	# prints elements starting from index 1 to 2 # prints tuple1[start_at : end_at-1]	(345, 3.2)
print tuple1[2:]	#prints tuple1 starting at index 2 till the end	(3.2, 'python', 3.14)
print tuple 2 * 2	# asterisk (*) -is the repetition operator. Prints the tuple2 two times.	(234, 'xyz', 234, 'xyz')
print tuple1 + tuple2	# prints concatenated tuples	('abcd', 345, 3.2,'python', 3.14, 234, 'xyz')

Q: *Write a program to create two tuples with various data types and print their values.*

Step 1: Open Jupyter Notebook.

Step 2: Create a new file.

Step 3: Rename the file (e.g., **tuple_example.ipynb**).

Step 4: In a new code cell, type the following code to create two tuples:

tuple1 = ('abcd', 345, 3.2, 'python', 3.14)

tuple2 = (234, 'xyz')

Step 5: Print the tuples using the print statement:

print(tuple1)

print(tuple2)

Output:

```
# tuple1 contains different data types
tuple1 = ('abcd', 345, 3.2, 'python', 3.14)

# tuple2 contains a number and a string
tuple2 = (234, 'xyz')


print(tuple1)
print(tuple2)

('abcd', 345, 3.2, 'python', 3.14)
(234, 'xyz')
```

2.2.3 Dictionary

A dictionary is an unordered collection of key-value pairs in Python. Each key must be unique and immutable, while the associated value can be of any data type. Dictionaries are defined using curly braces { }, and they allow efficient lookups based on keys.

dict1= {'name': 'ABCD' , 'code' : 6734 , 'dept' : 'Engg'} dict2= {}

dict2 ['rollno'] = "II-ITA24"

Code	Comment	Result
print dict1	# prints complete dictionary	{ 'dept': 'Engg', 'code':6734, 'name' : 'ABCD'}
print dict1.keys()	# prints all keys of dictionary	{ 'dept', 'code', 'name'}
print dict1.values	#prints all values of dictionary	{'Engg', 6734, 'ABCD'}
print dict2['rollno']	# print the value for the key rollno	II-ITA24

Q: *Write a program to create two dictionaries with key-value pairs and print their values.*

Step 1: Open Jupyter Notebook.

Step 2: Create a new file.

Step 3: Rename the file (e.g., **dictionary_example.ipynb**).

Step 4: In a new code cell, type the following code to create two dictionaries:

#dictionary1 = {'name': 'John', 'age': 25, 'height': 5.8}

\# dictionary2 = {'id': 101, 'course': 'Python'}

Step 5: Print the tuples using the **print** statement:

\# print(dictionary1)

\# print(dictionary2)

Output:

```
# dictionary1 contains key-value pairs of different data types
dictionary1 = {'name': 'John', 'age': 25, 'height': 5.8}

# dictionary2 contains a number and a string as values
dictionary2 = {'id': 101, 'course': 'Python'}

print(dictionary1)
print(dictionary2)

{'name': 'John', 'age': 25, 'height': 5.8}
{'id': 101, 'course': 'Python'}
```

2.2.4 Boolean Variables

Boolean variables in Python hold one of two values: True or False. These variables are typically used for logical operations, conditions, and controlling the flow of a program. They are crucial for decision-making constructs like if statements.

Q: *Write a program to create two boolean variables (True and False) and print their values.*

Step 1: Open Jupyter Notebook.

Step 2: Create a new file.

Step 3: Rename the file (e.g., **boolean_example.ipynb**).

Step 4: In a new code cell, type the following code to create two boolean variables:

\# bool1 − Truc

\# bool2 = False

Step 5: Print the tuples using the **print** statement:

\# print(bool1)

\# print(bool2)

Output:

```
▶ # boolean variable1 holds True
  bool1 = True

  # boolean variable2 holds False
  bool2 = False

  print(bool1)
  print(bool2)

  True
  False
```

Line Continuation in Python

In Python, long statements can be split across multiple lines using the backslash (\) to indicate line continuation. This is helpful for improving code readability, especially when dealing with complex expressions.

Q: *Write a program to calculate the total of three marks using line continuation and print a list of items without using line continuation.*

Step 1: Open Jupyter Notebook.

Step 2: Create a new file.

Step 3: Rename the file (e.g. **line_continuation_example.ipynb**).

Step 4: In a new **code cell,** type the following code to add marks:

mark1 = 85

mark2 = 90

mark3 = 78

Total = mark1 + \
        # mark2 + \
        # mark3

print("Total Marks:", Total)

```
▶ # Using line continuation to sum marks
  mark1 = 85
  mark2 = 90
  mark3 = 78

  Total = mark1 + \
          mark2 + \
          mark3

  print("Total Marks:", Total)

  Total Marks: 253
```

Step 5 : Create and Print a list that dose not require line continuation :

Output:

```
▶ Item = ['item1', 'item2', 'item3', 'item4', 'item5']

  print("Items List:", Item)

  Items List: ['item1', 'item2', 'item3', 'item4', 'item5']
```

2.3 Python Operators

Operators are special symbols in Python that carry out operations on variables and values. Python provides a rich set of operators, and each operator serves a unique purpose depending on the type of operation to be performed.

2.3.1 Types of Operator

Python language supports the following types of operators.

- Arithmetic Operators
- Comparison (Relational) Operators
- Assignment Operators
- Logical Operators
- Bitwise Operators
- Membership Operators
- Identity Operators
- Unary arithmetic Operators

2.3.1.1 Arithmetic Operations

Arithmetic operators in Python include addition (+), subtraction (-), multiplication (*), and division (/). These operators perform basic mathematical operations on numeric values and return a result.

Operator	Description
+ Addition	Adds two operands.
- Subtraction	Subtracts second operand from first operand.
* Multiplication	Multiplies two operands.
/ Division	Divides first operand by second operand.
% Modulus	Divides first operand by second operand and returns the remainder
** Exponent	Performs exponential (power) calculation
// Floor Division (Integer Division)	Division of operands in which the quotient without fraction is returned as a result.

Q: Write a Python program to perform addition, subtraction, multiplication, and division with two numbers and print the results.

Step 1: Open Jupyter Notebook.

Step 2: Create a new file.

Step 3: Rename the file (e.g. **arithmetic_example.ipynb**).

Step 4: In a new **code cell,** type the following code to create two boolean variables:

mark1 = 85

mark2 = 90

mark3 = 78

Total = mark1 + \
        # mark2 + \
        # mark3

print("Total Marks:", Total)

Step 5: Print the tuples using the **print** statement:

Item = ['item1', 'item2', 'item3', 'item4', 'item5']
print("Items List:", Item)

```
# Using line continuation to sum marks
mark1 = 85
mark2 = 90
mark3 = 78

Total = mark1 + \
        mark2 + \
        mark3

print("Total Marks:", Total)

Total Marks: 253
```

Step 6 : Print a list that dose not require line continuation :

Item = ['item1', 'item2', 'item3', 'item4', 'item5']
print("Items List:", Item)

Output:

```
Item = ['item1', 'item2', 'item3', 'item4', 'item5']

print("Items List:", Item)

Items List: ['item1', 'item2', 'item3', 'item4', 'item5']
```

2.3.1.2 Comparison Operators

Python's comparison operators (==, !=, >, <, >=, <=) are used to compare two values. They return a boolean value (True or False) based on whether the condition is met, enabling decision-making in the code.

Operator	Description
==	If the values of two operands are equal, then this operator returns true.
!=	If values of two operands are not equal, then this operator returns true.
>	If the value of first operand is strictly greater than the value of second operand, then this operator returns true.

<	If the value of first operand is strictly smaller than the value of second operand, then this operator returns true.	
>=	If the value of first operand is greater than or equal to the value of second operand, then this operator returns true.	
<=	If the value of first operand is smaller than or equal to the value of second operand, then this operator returns true.	

Q: Write a Python program to check if two numbers are equal, not equal, greater than, less than, greater than or equal to, and less than or equal to. .

Step 1: Open Jupyter Notebook.

Step 2: Create a new file.

Step 3: Rename the file (e.g. **arithmetic_example.ipynb**).

Step 4: In a new **code cell,** type the following code to define two numbers:

```
# a = 10
# b = 5
```

Step 5: Perform comparison operations:

```
# equal = a == b
# not_equal = a != b
# greater_than = a > b
# less_than = a < b
# greater_or_equal = a >= b
# less_or_equal = a <= b
```

Step 5: Print the results of the comparisons:

```
# print("Equal:", equal)
# print("Not Equal:", not_equal)
# print("Greater Than:", greater_than)
# print("Less Than:", less_than)
# print("Greater or Equal:", greater_or_equal)
# print("Less or Equal:", less_or_equal)
```

Step 7: Run the code by pressing Shift + Enter or clicking the Run button.

Output:

```python
a = 10
b = 5

equal = a == b                  # Check if a is equal to b
not_equal = a != b              # Check if a is not equal to b
greater_than = a > b            # Check if a is greater than b
less_than = a < b               # Check if a is less than b
greater_or_equal = a >= b       # Check if a is greater than or equal to b
less_or_equal = a <= b          # Check if a is less than or equal to b

print("Equal:", equal)
print("Not Equal:", not_equal)
print("Greater Than:", greater_than)
print("Less Than:", less_than)
print("Greater or Equal:", greater_or_equal)
print("Less or Equal:", less_or_equal)
```

```
Equal: False
Not Equal: True
Greater Than: True
Less Than: False
Greater or Equal: True
Less or Equal: False
```

2.3.1.3 Assignment Operators

Assignment operators (+=, -=, *=, /=, etc.) are shorthand operators that combine an operation with assignment. They modify the value of a variable in place, making the code more concise and readable.

=	Assigns values from right side operand to left side operand.
+=	Performs addition using two operands and assigns the result to left side operand.
-=	Subtracts right side operand from the left side operand and assigns the result to left side operand.
*=	Performs multiplication using two operands and assigns the result to left side operand.
/=	Divides left side operand by the right side operand and assigns the result to left side operand.
%=	Finds modulus using two operands and assigns the result to left side operand.
**=	Performs exponential calculation and assigns the result to the left side operand.
//=	Performs floor division and assigns the result to the left side operand

Q: Python Program for Assignment Operators

Step 1: Open Jupyter Notebook.

Step 2: Create a new file.

Step 3: Rename the file (e.g., **assignment_example.ipynb**).

Step 4: In a new code cell, type the following code to define a variable:

x = 10

Step 5: Perform various assignment operations:

x += 5 # Equivalent to x = x + 5

x -= 2 # Equivalent to x = x - 2

x *= 3 # Equivalent to x = x * 3

x /= 2 # Equivalent to x = x / 2

x //= 2 # Equivalent to x = x // 2 (floor division)

x **= 2 # Equivalent to x = x ** 2 (exponentiation)

x %= 3 # Equivalent to x = x % 3 (modulus)

Step 6: Print the results of the assignments:

print("Final value of x:", x)

Step 7: Run the code by pressing Shift + Enter or clicking the Run button.

Output:

```
x=10

# Perform assignment operations
x += 5     # Equivalent to x = x + 5
x -= 2     # Equivalent to x = x - 2
x *= 3     # Equivalent to x = x * 3
x /= 2     # Equivalent to x = x / 2
x //= 2    # Equivalent to x = x // 2 (floor division)
x **= 2    # Equivalent to x = x ** 2 (exponentiation)
x %= 3     # Equivalent to x = x % 3 (modulus)

# Print the final value of x
print("Final value of x:", x)

Final value of x: 0.0
```

2.3.1.4 Logical Operators

Logical operators in Python include and, or, and not. These operators are used to combine or negate boolean expressions. and returns True if both operands are True, or returns True if at least one is True, and not inverts the boolean value.

Following table shows all the logical operators supported by python:

Operator	Description
and	Logical AND returns true, if and only if both operands are true.
or	Logical OR returns true, if any of the two operands is true.

not	Logical NOT returns the logical negation of its operand.

Q: Write a Python program to demonstrate the use of logical operators. Use two boolean variables and apply logical AND, OR, and NOT operations, then print the results.

Step 1: Open Jupyter Notebook.

Step 2: Create a new file.

Step 3: Rename the file (e.g., logical_example.ipynb).

Step 4: In a new code cell, type the following code to define two boolean variables:

a = True
b = False

Step 5: Perform logical operations:

logical_and = a and b

logical_or = a or b

logical_not_a = not a

logical_not_b = not b

Step 6: Print the results of the logical operations:

print("Logical AND (a and b):", logical_and)
print("Logical OR (a or b):", logical_or)
print("Logical NOT (not a):", logical_not_a)
print("Logical NOT (not b):", logical_not_b)

Output:

```
# Define two boolean variables
a = True
b = False

# Perform logical operations
logical_and = a and b          # Logical AND
logical_or = a or b            # Logical OR
logical_not_a = not a          # Logical NOT on a
logical_not_b = not b          # Logical NOT on b

# Print the results
print("Logical AND (a and b):", logical_and)
print("Logical OR (a or b):", logical_or)
print("Logical NOT (not a):", logical_not_a)
print("Logical NOT (not b):", logical_not_b)


Logical AND (a and b): False
Logical OR (a or b): True
Logical NOT (not a): False
Logical NOT (not b): True
```

2.3.1.5 Bitwise Operators

Bitwise operators perform operations on the binary representations of integers. They include & (AND), | (OR), ^ (XOR), ~ (NOT), as well as bitwise shift operators (<<, >>) for manipulating individual bits.

Operator	Description
&	Performs Bitwise AND operation between two the operands.
|	Performs Bitwise OR operation between two the operands.
^	Performs Bitwise XOR (exclusive OR) operation between two the operands.
~	Performs Bitwise 1's complement on a single operand.
<<	Shifts the first operand left by the number of bits specified by the second operand (Bitwise Left Shift).
>>	Shifts the first operand right by the number of bits specified by the second operand (Bitwise Right Shift).

Q: Write a Python program to demonstrate the use of bitwise operators. Use an integer variable and apply bitwise AND, OR, XOR, NOT, left shift, and right shift operations, then print the results.

Step 1: Open Jupyter Notebook.

Step 2: Create a new file.

Step 3: Rename the file (e.g., bitwise_example.ipynb).

Step 4: In a new code cell, type the following code to define an integer variable:

num1 = 10
num2 = 4

Step 5: Perform bitwise operations:

bitwise_and = num & num2

bitwise_or = num | num2

bitwise_xor = num ^ num2

bitwise_not = ~num

left_shift = num << 1

right_shift = num >> 1

Step 6: Print the results of the bitwise operations:

print("Bitwise AND (num & num2):", bitwise_and)

print("Bitwise OR (num | num2):", bitwise_or)

print("Bitwise XOR (num ^ num2):", bitwise_xor)

print("Bitwise NOT (~num):", bitwise_not)

print("Left Shift (num << 1):", left_shift)

print("Right Shift (num >> 1):", right_shift)

Output:

```
▶ # Define an integer variable
  num = 10  # Binary: 1010
  num2 = 4  # Binary: 0100

  # Perform bitwise operations
  bitwise_and = num & num2         # Bitwise AND
  bitwise_or = num | num2          # Bitwise OR
  bitwise_xor = num ^ num2         # Bitwise XOR
  bitwise_not = ~num               # Bitwise NOT
  left_shift = num << 1            # Left shift
  right_shift = num >> 1           # Right shift

  # Print the results
  print("Bitwise AND (num & num2):", bitwise_and)
  print("Bitwise OR (num | num2):", bitwise_or)
  print("Bitwise XOR (num ^ num2):", bitwise_xor)
  print("Bitwise NOT (~num):", bitwise_not)
  print("Left Shift (num << 1):", left_shift)
  print("Right Shift (num >> 1):", right_shift)


  Bitwise AND (num & num2): 0
  Bitwise OR (num | num2): 14
  Bitwise XOR (num ^ num2): 14
  Bitwise NOT (~num): -11
  Left Shift (num << 1): 20
  Right Shift (num >> 1): 5
```

2.3.1.6 Membership Operators

Membership operators in and not in check for the presence or absence of a value within a sequence such as a list or string. in returns True if the value is found, while not in returns True if it is not.

Operator	Description
in	Evaluates to true if it finds a variable in the specified sequence and false otherwise.
not in	Evaluates to true if it does not finds a variable in the specified sequence and false otherwise.

Step 1: Open Jupyter Notebook.

Step 2: Create a new file.

Step 3: Rename the file (e.g., membership_example.ipynb).

Step 4: In a new code cell, type the following code to define a list:

fruits = ['apple', 'banana', 'cherry', 'date']

Step 5: Check for the presence of specific fruits using membership operators:

is_in = 'banana' in fruits

\# is_not_in = 'orange' not in fruits

Step 7: Run the code by pressing Shift + Enter or clicking the Run button.

Output:

```
# Define a list of fruits
fruits = ['apple', 'banana', 'cherry', 'date']

# Check membership
is_in = 'banana' in fruits          # Check if 'banana' is in the list
is_not_in = 'orange' not in fruits  # Check if 'orange' is not in the list

# Print the results
print("'banana' in fruits:", is_in)
print("'orange' not in fruits:", is_not_in)


'banana' in fruits: True
'orange' not in fruits: True
```

2.3.1.7 Identity Operators

Identity operators is and is not are used to check if two variables refer to the same object in memory. is returns True if they are the same object, while is not returns True if they are not.

Operator	Description
is	Returns true if both operands point to the same object and false otherwise.
is not	Returns false if both operands point to the same object and true otherwise.

Q: Write a Python program to demonstrate the use of identity operators is and is not. Create two variables and check if they refer to the same object in memory.

Step 1: Open Jupyter Notebook.

Step 2: Create a new file.

Step 3: Rename the file (e.g., identity_example.ipynb).

Step 4: In a new code cell, type the following code to create two variables:

\# a = [1, 2, 3]
\# b = a
\# c = [1, 2, 3]

Step 5: Use identity operators to check if the variables refer to the same object:

\# is_same = (a is b)
\# is_not_same = (a is not c)

Step 6: Print the results of the identity checks:
\# is_same = (a is b)

\# is_not_same = (a is not c)

Step 7: Run the code by pressing Shift + Enter or clicking the Run button.

Output:

```
H  # Create two variables
   a = [1, 2, 3]
   b = a                        # Variable b refers to the same object as a
   c = [1, 2, 3]                # Variable c is a new object with the same content

   # Check identity
   is_same = (a is b)           # Check if a and b refer to the same object
   is_not_same = (a is not c)   # Check if a and c do not refer to the same object

   # Print the results
   print("a is b:", is_same)
   print("a is not c:", is_not_same)

   a is b: True
   a is not c: True
```

2.3.1.8 Unary Operators

Unary operators operate on a single operand. In Python, the unary + and - operators are used to indicate positive and negative values, respectively. For example, +num leaves the number unchanged, while -num negates it.

Operator	Description
+	Returns its numeric argument without any change.
-	Returns its numeric argument with its sign changed.

*Q: Write a Python program to demonstrate the use of unary arithmetic operators. Use the unary **+** and **–** operators on a variable.*

Step 1: Open Jupyter Notebook.

Step 2: Create a new file.

Step 3: Rename the file (e.g., unary_arithmetic_example.ipynb).

Step 4: In a new code cell, type the following code to create a variable:

\# num = 10

Step 5: Use unary arithmetic operators to demonstrate their functionality:

\# positive_num = +num

\# negative_num = -num

Step 6: Print the results of the unary operations:

\# print("Original Number:", num)

\# print("Using Unary +:", positive_num)

\# print("Using Unary -:", negative_num)

Output:

```
# Create a variable
num = 10
# Unary operators
positive_num = +num       # Unary + operator (no effect on positive number)
negative_num = -num       # Unary - operator (negates the number)

# Print the results
print("Original Number:", num)
print("Using Unary +:", positive_num)
print("Using Unary -:", negative_num)

Original Number: 10
Using Unary +: 10
Using Unary -: -10
```

2.4 FUNCTIONS

A function is a group of statements that perform a specific task. If a program is large, it is difficult to understand the steps involved in it. Hence, it is subdivided into a number of smaller programs called subprograms or modules. Each subprogram specifies one or more actions to be performed for the larger program. Such subprograms are called as functions. Functions may or may not take arguments and may or may not produce results.

Advantages of Functions

- Decomposing larger programs in to smaller functions makes program easy to understand, maintain and debug.

- Functions developed for one program can be reused with or without modification when needed.

- Reduces program development time and cost.

- It is easy to locate and isolate faulty function.

2.4.1 Types of functions

2.4.1.1 Built-in/Pre-defined function

Python provides several built-in functions like len() (returns the length of a list), type() (returns the data type of a variable), and sum() (returns the sum of all elements in an iterable). These functions are essential for performing common operations efficiently.

Example:

print()	Print objects to the stream.
input()	Reads a line from input, converts it to a string (stripping a trailing newline), and returns that.
abs()	Return the absolute value of a number.
len()	Return the length (the number of items) of an object.

Q: Write a Python program to create a list of numbers and use built-in functions to find the length, type, and sum of the list. Print the results.

Step 1: Open Jupyter Notebook.

Step 2: Create a new file.

Step 3: Rename the file (e.g., built_in_functions_example.ipynb).

Step 4: In a new code cell, type the following code to create a list:

numbers = [1, 2, 3, 4, 5]

Step 5: Use built-in functions to demonstrate their functionality:

length_of_list = len(numbers)

type_of_list = type(numbers)

sum_of_list = sum(numbers)

Step 6: Print the results of the built-in function calls:

print("Length of list:", length_of_list)

print("Type of variable:", type_of_list)

print("Sum of list elements:", sum_of_list)

Step 7: Run the code by pressing Shift + Enter or clicking the Run button.

Output:

```
# Create a list
numbers = [1, 2, 3, 4, 5]

# Use built-in functions
length_of_list = len(numbers)          # Get the length of the list
type_of_list = type(numbers)           # Get the type of the variable
sum_of_list = sum(numbers)             # Calculate the sum of the list elements

# Print the results
print("Length of list:", length_of_list)
print("Type of variable:", type_of_list)
print("Sum of list elements:", sum_of_list)

Length of list: 5
Type of variable: <class 'list'>
Sum of list elements: 15
```

UNIT 3 - CONTROL FLOW, FUNCTIONS

3.1 Boolean Values and Operators

Boolean values (True or False) are used in Python for logical operations. Relational operators like ==, !=, >, and < compare values and return Boolean results. Logical operators (and, or, not) combine or modify Boolean values to evaluate multiple conditions.

The following examples use the operator !=, which compares two operands and produces True if they are not equal and False otherwise:

```
>>> 5 != 5
True
>>> 5 != 6
False
```

So, True and False are special values which belong to the Boolean type; they are not strings (case sensitive):

To know the type of data, the following example can be used.

```
>>> type(True)
<type 'bool'>
>>> type(False)
<type 'bool'>
```

The relational operators are as follows: x == y

```
                    # x is equal to y
x != y              # x is not equal to y
x > y               # x is greater than y
x < y               # x is less than y
x >= y              # x is greater than or equal to y
x <= y              # x is less than or equal to y
```

Q: Write a Python program that uses Boolean values and operators to compare two variables. The program should demonstrate the use of relational operators (==, !=, >, <) and logical operators (and, or, not).

Step 1: Open Jupyter Notebook.

Step 2: Click on a new **code cell** to start typing.

Step 3: Write the following code to demonstrate Boolean values and operators:

```
# x = 10 # Assigning values to variables
# y = 20
```

equal = (x == y) # *Relational operators*

not_equal = (x != y)

greater_than = (x > y)

less_than = (x < y)

and_operator = (x < y and x != y) # *Logical operators*

or_operator = (x == y or x < y)

not_operator = not(x == y)

Step 4: Print the results of the unary operations:

print("Equal:", equal)

print("Not Equal:", not_equal)

print("Greater Than:", greater_than)

print("Less Than:", less_than)

print("AND Operator:", and_operator)

print("OR Operator:", or_operator)

print("NOT Operator:", not_operator)

Output:

```
# Example of Boolean values and relational operators

# Assigning values to variables
x = 10
y = 20

# Relational operators
equal = (x == y)        # Checks if x is equal to y
not_equal = (x != y)    # Checks if x is not equal to y
greater_than = (x > y)  # Checks if x is greater than y
less_than = (x < y)     # Checks if x is less than y

# Logical operators
and_operator = (x < y and x != y)   # Checks if both conditions are true
or_operator = (x == y or x < y)     # Checks if either condition is true
not_operator = not(x == y)          # Negates the result

# Print the results
print("Equal:", equal)
print("Not Equal:", not_equal)
print("Greater Than:", greater_than)
print("Less Than:", less_than)
print("AND Operator:", and_operator)
print("OR Operator:", or_operator)
print("NOT Operator:", not_operator)


Equal: False
Not Equal: True
Greater Than: False
Less Than: True
AND Operator: True
OR Operator: True
NOT Operator: True
```

3.2 Condition Statements

3.2.1 If Statements

An *if* statement is a conditional structure that executes a block of code if a specified condition is True. It allows for decision-making in programs, where different actions are performed based on different conditions.

Syntax :

if test expression: *(or)*   if test expression: statement
satement(s)

The program evaluates the test expression and will execute statement(s) only if the text expression is True. If the text expression is False, the statement(s) is not executed.

Q: Write a Python program that uses Boolean values and operators to compare two variables. The program should demonstrate the use of relational operators (==, !=, >, <) and logical operators (and, or, not).

Step 1: Open Jupyter Notebook.

Step 2: Click on a new code cell to start typing.

Step 3: Rename the file (e.g., if_statement_example.ipynb).

Step 4: In a new code cell, type the following code to create a conditional check using the `if` statement.

num = 10

if num > 5:

print("The number is greater than 5.")
if num == 10:

print("The number is equal to 10.")

if num < 15:

print("The number is less than 15.")

Step 5: Run the code by pressing Shift + Enter or clicking the Run button.

Output:

```
num = 10

if num > 5:
    print("The number is greater than 5.")

if num == 10:
    print("The number is equal to 10.")

if num < 15:
    print("The number is less than 15.")


The number is greater than 5.
The number is equal to 10.
The number is less than 15.
```

3.2.2 If-Else Statements

The **if...else** statement is called **alternative execution**, in which there are two possibilities and the condition determines which one gets executed. The syntax of if...else statement is given below.

Syntax of if...else :

    if test expression:
        Body of if else:
        Body of else

The if...else statement evaluates the test expression and will execute body of if only when test condition is True. And if the condition is False, body of else is executed. Indentation is used to separate the blocks.

Q : Write a Python program that checks if a person is eligible to vote using an if...else statement.

[NOTE: A person is eligible to vote if their age is 18 or older; otherwise, they are not eligible.]

Step 1: Open Jupyter Notebook.

Step 2: Click on a new code cell to start typing.

Step 3: Rename the file (e.g., if_else_example.ipynb).

Step 4: In a new code cell, assign a value to the variable age.

age = 20

Step 5: Use an if statement to check if the age is 18 or greater.

if age >= 18:

print("You are eligible to vote.")

Step 6: Use an else statement to handle cases where the age is less than 18.

else:

print("You are not eligible to vote.")

Step 7: Print the appropriate message for voting eligibility based on the condition.

Step 8: Run the code by pressing Shift + Enter or clicking the Run button.

Output:

```
▶ # Assign a value to the variable age
  age = 20

  # Check if the age is 18 or greater
  if age >= 18:
      print("You are eligible to vote.")

  # If the age is less than 18
  else:
      print("You are not eligible to vote.")


  You are eligible to vote.
```

Q : Write a Python program that assigns a grade to a student based on their score.

Step 1: Open Jupyter Notebook.

Step 2: Click on a new code cell to start typing.

Step 3: Rename the file (e.g., student_grade_example.ipynb).

Step 4: In a new code cell, assign a value to the variable score.

score = 85

Step 5: Use an if statement to check if the score is greater than or equal to 90 (grade A).

if score >= 90:

print("Grade: A")

Step 6: Use an elif statement to check if the score is between 80 and 89 (grade B).

elif score >= 80:

print("Grade: B")

Step 7: Use another elif to check if the score is between 70 and 79 (grade C).

elif score >= 70:

print("Grade: C")

Step 8: Use another elif to check if the score is between 60 and 69 (grade D).

elif score >= 60:

print("Grade: D")

Step 9: Use an else statement to assign an F grade for scores below 60.

else:

print("Grade: F")

Step 10: Print the grade based on the condition.

Step 11: Run the code by pressing Shift + Enter or clicking the Run button.

Output:

```
▶  # Assign a value to the variable score
   score = 85

   # Check if the score is 90 or above
   if score >= 90:
       print("Grade: A")

   # Check if the score is between 80 and 89
   elif score >= 80:
       print("Grade: B")

   # Check if the score is between 70 and 79
   elif score >= 70:
       print("Grade: C")

   # Check if the score is between 60 and 69
   elif score >= 60:
       print("Grade: D")

   # Assign F grade for scores below 60
   else:
       print("Grade: F")

   Grade: B
```

3.2.3 Chained Conditionals (If-Elif and Else Statements)

The elif (else-if) and else statements extend an if statement to handle multiple conditions. elif checks another condition if the first is False, and else defines a block to execute if no conditions are met.

Syntax of if...elif...else

```
if test expression:
    # Body of if
elif test expression:
    # Body of elif else
elif test expression:
    # Body of else
```

The example explains the if-elif-else: if x < y:

```
print 'x is less than y' elif x > y:
print 'x is greater than y' else:
print 'x and y are equal'
```

Q : Write a Python program that checks if a number is positive, negative, or zero using an if elif and else statement.

Step 1: Open Jupyter Notebook.

Step 2: Click on a new code cell to start typing.

Step 3: Rename the file (e.g., condition_example.ipynb).

Step 4: In a new code cell, assign a value to a variable, **num.**

\# num = 10

Step 5: Use an if statement to check if the number is positive.

\# if num > 0:

\#   print("The number is positive.")

Step 6: Use an elif statement to check if the number is negative.

\# elif num < 0:

\#   print("The number is negative.")

Step 7: Use an else statement to check if the number is zero.

\# else:

\#   print("The number is zero.")

Step 8: Run the code by pressing Shift + Enter or clicking the Run button.

Output :

```python
# Assign a value to the variable num
num = 10

# Check if the number is positive
if num > 0:
    print("The number is positive.")

# Check if the number is negative
elif num < 0:
    print("The number is negative.")

# Check if the number is zero
else:
    print("The number is zero.")


The number is positive.
```

3.2.3 Nested Conditionals

Nested conditionals involve placing an if statement inside another if or else block. This structure allows for more complex decision-making, where a second condition is evaluated only if the first is satisfied.

Syntax :

    if test expression:

        Body of if else:

        if test expression:

        Body of if else:

        if test expression:

        Body of if:

      Else:

      Body of else

Q : Write a program that checks if a person qualifies for a discount based on their age and membership status using nested conditionals.

Step 1: Open Jupyter Notebook.

Step 2: Click on a new code cell to start typing.

Step 3: Rename the file (e.g., nested_conditional_discount_check.ipynb).

Step 4: In a new code cell, assign values to age and is_member.

```python
# age = 65  # Assigning age

# is_member = True  # Membership status
```

Step 4: Use an if statement to check if the person's age is 60 or above.

Step 5: Inside the if, use another if statement to check if the person is a member and print a message about the discount.

Step 6: Use an else statement to check if the person is a member and under 60 to offer another type of discount.

Step 7: If none of the conditions are met, print that the person does not qualify for any discounts.

```python
# if age >= 60:
#    if is_member:
#        print("Eligible for senior citizen member discount.")
#    else:
#        print("Eligible for senior citizen discount.")
# else:
#    if is_member:
#        print("Eligible for member discount.")
#    else:
#        print("No discount available.")
```

Step 8: Run the code by pressing Shift + Enter or clicking the Run button.

Output:

```
age = 65   # Assigning age
is_member = True   # Membership status

if age >= 60:
    if is_member:
        print("Eligible for senior citizen member discount.")
    else:
        print("Eligible for senior citizen discount.")
else:
    if is_member:
        print("Eligible for member discount.")
    else:
        print("No discount available.")


Eligible for senior citizen member discount.
```

3.3 Looping Statements

Looping statements in programming are used to execute a block of code repeatedly as long as a specified condition is true. These are fundamental constructs in most programming languages and help automate repetitive tasks by controlling the flow of execution.

3.3.1 For Loops

A for loop in Python iterates over a sequence (like a list or range) and executes a block of code repeatedly for each element in the sequence. This is useful for performing repetitive tasks or iterating over collections.

The syntax for a for loop in Python is as follows:

for variable in sequence:

Code block to execute for each item in the sequence

- *variable:* This is the loop variable that takes on the value of each item in the sequence (e.g., a list, tuple, string, or range) during each iteration.
- *sequence:* This is the collection of items (such as a list, tuple, string, or range()) that the loop will iterate over.
- *Code block:* The indented block of code that will be executed once for each item in the sequence.

Q : Write a program that checks if a person qualifies for a discount based on their age and membership status using nested conditionals.

Step 1: Open Jupyter Notebook.

Step 2: Click on a new code cell to start typing.

Step 3: Rename the file (e.g., iteration_variable_state.ipynb).

Step 4: In a new code cell, initialize a variable (e.g., count = 0).

count = 0

Step 5: Use a for loop to iterate over a range of values and reassign the variable in each iteration.

\# for i in range(5):

\#   count = count + 1 # Reassigning variable with new value

Step 6: Print the value of the variable inside the loop to observe how it changes with each assignment.

\#   print("Iteration", i + 1, "- Count:", count)

Step 7: Run the code to observe the variable's state across iterations.

Output :

```
count = 0   # Initializing the variable

for i in range(5):
    count = count + 1   # Reassigning variable with new value
    print("Iteration", i + 1, "- Count:", count)


Iteration 1 - Count: 1
Iteration 2 - Count: 2
Iteration 3 - Count: 3
Iteration 4 - Count: 4
Iteration 5 - Count: 5
```

3.3.2 While Loops

A while loop continues executing as long as its condition remains True. It is commonly used when the number of iterations is not predetermined, making it different from the for loop.

The syntax for a while loop in Python is as follows:

> while condition:
>
> > \# Code block to execute repeatedly

- *Condition:* This is the logical expression that is evaluated before each iteration. If the condition is True, the loop's code block is executed. If the condition becomes False, the loop stops.
- *Code block:* The indented block of code inside the loop is executed as long as the condition remains true.

Q : Write a program that checks if a person qualifies for a discount based on their age and membership status using nested conditionals.

Step 1: Open Jupyter Notebook.

Step 2: Click on a new code cell to start typing.

Step 3: Rename the file (e.g., while_loop_example.ipynb).

Step 4: In a new code cell, initialize a variable.

\# i = 1

Step 5: Create a while loop with a condition to keep looping as long as i is less than or equal to 5.

\# while i <= 5:

Step 6: Print the value of i in each iteration and increment it.

print(i) # i += 1

Step 7: Run the code to observe the output.

Output :

```
i = 1  # Initializing the variable

while i <= 5:
    print(i)
    i += 1  # Increment the variable



1
2
3
4
5
```

3.3.3 Nested Loops

Nested loops occur when one loop is placed inside another. In Python, they are often used for tasks like generating matrices or tables, where each combination of outer and inner loop values is processed.

The syntax for a nested loop:

```
for outer_variable in outer_sequence:
# Outer loop code block
for inner_variable in inner_sequence:
# Inner loop code block
```

- **Outer loop**: This runs first, and for each iteration of the outer loop, the inner loop is executed.
- **Inner loop**: This is a loop that runs for each iteration of the outer loop.

Q : Write a program that prints a multiplication table using nested loops.

Step 1: Open Jupyter Notebook.

Step 2: Click on a new code cell to start typing.

Step 3: Rename the file   (e.g., nested_loop_example.ipynb).

Step 4: In a new code cell, create an outer loop to represent the rows of the multiplication table.

for i in range(1, 6):

Step 5: Create an inner loop to represent the columns of the multiplication table.

for j in range(1, 6):

Step 6: Print the result of multiplying the row and column indices.

\# print(i * j, end=' ')

\# print()

Step 7: Run the code to observe the multiplication table output.

Output :

```
for i in range(1, 6):   # Outer loop for rows
    for j in range(1, 6):   # Inner loop for columns
        print(i * j, end=' ')   # Print the product
    print()   # New line after each row


1 2 3 4 5
2 4 6 8 10
3 6 9 12 15
4 8 12 16 20
5 10 15 20 25
```

3.3.4 List Iteration

In Python, lists can be iterated using a for loop, where each element of the list is accessed sequentially. This allows for operations such as printing or modifying elements within the loop.

Q : Write a program that prints each item in a list using a for loop.

Step 1: Open Jupyter Notebook.

Step 2: Click on a new code cell to start typing.

Step 3: Rename the file (e.g., for_loop_example.ipynb).

Step 4: In a new code cell, create a list of items (e.g., items = ['apple', 'banana', 'cherry']).

\# items = ['apple', 'banana', 'cherry'] # Initializing the list

Step 5: Create a for loop to iterate through the list and print each item.

\# for item in items:

\# print(item)

Step 6: Run the code to observe the output.

Output:

```
items = ['apple', 'banana', 'cherry']  # Initializing the list

for item in items:
    print(item)  # Print each item in the list


apple
banana
cherry
```

3.4 Continue, Break, and Pass Statements

3.4.1 Continue

- The continue statement is used to skip the rest of the code inside the loop for the current iteration and immediately move to the next iteration.
- It is typically used when you want to skip certain conditions within a loop but still continue the looping process.

Syntax:

```
python
Copy code
for i in range(5):
    if i == 3:
        continue  # Skips the iteration when i is 3
    print(i)
```

3.4.2 Break

- The break statement is used to exit the loop entirely, regardless of the iteration or condition. Once break is encountered, the loop terminates.
- It is useful for stopping a loop prematurely when a condition is met.

Syntax:

```
for i in range(5):
if i == 3:
break # Exits the loop when i is 3
print(i)
```

3.4.3 Pass

- The pass statement does nothing and is used as a placeholder where code is required syntactically but you don't want any operation to happen.
- It is often used during development to define loops or functions that you plan to implement later.

Syntax:

```
for i in range(5):

    if i == 3:

        pass  # Does nothing when i is 3
```

```
        print(i)
```

Q : Write a Python program to manage a queue of people waiting for tickets. The program should:

1. *Skip over a person who doesn't have enough money using the continue statement.*
2. *Stop the process when the tickets are sold out using the break statement.*
3. *Handle an unknown person (name as "Unknown") using the pass statement, without performing any action.*

Step 1: Open Jupyter Notebook.

Step 2: Click on a new code cell to start typing.

Step 3: Rename the file (e.g., ticket_queue_example.ipynb).

Step 4: Initialize a list of people waiting in line, along with their corresponding money and the tickets.

```python
# people_in_queue = [("John", 50), ("Alice", 20), ("Unknown", 100), ("Bob", 5), ("Charlie", 50)]
# ticket_price = 20
# tickets_left = 3
```

Step 5: In a new code cell, create a loop to iterate through the queue.

Step 6: Inside the loop:

- Use *continue* to skip a person if they don't have enough money.
- Use *break* to stop the process if the tickets are sold out.
- Use *pass* for a person with the name "Unknown" without performing any action.

```python
# for person, money in people_in_queue:  # Iterate over the queue of people
#    if person == "Unknown":
#        pass  # Do nothing if the person's name is "Unknown"
#    elif money < ticket_price:
#        print(f"{person} doesn't have enough money for the ticket.")
#        continue  # Skip to the next person if they don't have enough money
#    elif tickets_left == 0:
#        print("Tickets are sold out!")
#        break  # Stop the process if tickets are sold out
#    else:
#        print(f"{person} bought a ticket.")
#        tickets_left -= 1  # Reduce the number of tickets available
```

Step 7: Run the code and observe the results.

Output:

```
▶ people_in_queue = [("John", 50), ("Alice", 20), ("Unknown", 100), ("Bob", 5), ("Charlie", 50)]
  ticket_price = 20
  tickets_left = 3

  for person, money in people_in_queue:  # Iterate over the queue of people
      if person == "Unknown":
          pass  # Do nothing if the person's name is "Unknown"
      elif money < ticket_price:
          print(f"{person} doesn't have enough money for the ticket.")
          continue  # Skip to the next person if they don't have enough money
      elif tickets_left == 0:
          print("Tickets are sold out!")
          break  # Stop the process if tickets are sold out
      else:
          print(f"{person} bought a ticket.")
          tickets_left -= 1  # Reduce the number of tickets available


  John bought a ticket.
  Alice bought a ticket.
  Bob doesn't have enough money for the ticket.
  Charlie bought a ticket.
```

3.5 Input Function

he input() function is one of Python's built-in functions that allows programs to gather input from the user. This input is always treated as a string, no matter what the user enters, but it can be converted into other data types (e.g., integers or floats) if necessary. The function pauses the program's execution until the user provides the input and presses Enter.

Syntax:

```
# variable = input("Enter your input: ")
```

Q : Write a Python program that collects student details (name, age, and grade)

Step 1: Open Jupyter Notebook.

Step 2: Click on a new code cell to start typing.

Step 3: Rename the file (e.g., student_details_example.ipynb).

Step 3: In a new code cell, prompt the user to enter their name, age, and grade using the input() function.

```
# student_name = input("Enter your name: ")  # Get the student's name

# student_age = input("Enter your age: ")    # Get the student's age

# student_grade = input("Enter your grade: ")  # Get the student's grade
```

Step 4: Print the entered student details.

```
# print("Student Details:")  # Print a message

# print("Name:", student_name)  # Display the student's name

# print("Age:", student_age)    # Display the student's age

# print("Grade:", student_grade)  # Display the student's grade
```

Step 5: Run the code by pressing Shift + Enter or clicking the Run button.

Output :

```
student_name = input("Enter your name: ")  # Get the student's name
student_age = input("Enter your age: ")     # Get the student's age
student_grade = input("Enter your grade: ")  # Get the student's grade

print("Student Details:")  # Print a message
print("Name:", student_name)  # Display the student's name
print("Age:", student_age)    # Display the student's age
print("Grade:", student_grade)  # Display the student's grade


Enter your name: John
Enter your age: 10

Enter your grade: 5
```

```
student_name = input("Enter your name: ")  # Get the student's name
student_age = input("Enter your age: ")     # Get the student's age
student_grade = input("Enter your grade: ")  # Get the student's grade

print("Student Details:")  # Print a message
print("Name:", student_name)  # Display the student's name
print("Age:", student_age)    # Display the student's age
print("Grade:", student_grade)  # Display the student's grade

Enter your name: John
Enter your age: 10
Enter your grade: 5
Student Details:
Name: John
Age: 10
Grade: 5
```

3.6 Recursion

Recursion is a programming technique where a function calls itself to solve a problem by breaking it down into smaller subproblems. This self-referential approach continues until a base case, or termination condition, is met, which stops the recursion. Each recursive call processes a subset of the original problem, gradually leading to a solution.

Advantages of recursion

(1) Recursive functions make the code look clean and elegant.

(2) A complex task can be broken down into simpler sub-problems using recursion.

(3) Sequence generation is easier with recursion than using some nested iteration.

Disadvantages of recursion

(1) Sometimes the logic behind recursion is hard to follow through.

(2) Recursive calls are expensive (inefficient) as they take up a lot of memory and time.

(3) Recursive functions are hard to debug.

Q : Write a Python program that uses recursion to calculate the nth Fibonacci number.

Step 1: Open Jupyter Notebook.

Step 2: Click on a new code cell to start typing.

Step 3: Rename the file (e.g., fibonacci_recursion_example.ipynb).

Step 4: Define a recursive function named fibonacci(n) that returns the nth Fibonacci number.

def fibonacci(n): # Define a function to calculate Fibonacci numbers

if n <= 0:

return 0

elif n == 1:

return 1

else: # Recursive case

return fibonacci(n - 1) + fibonacci(n - 2)

Step 5: Call the function and print the result for a given value of n.

n = 5 # Set the value of n

print(f"The {n}th Fibonacci number is: {fibonacci(n)}")

Output :

```
def fibonacci(n):  # Define a function to calculate Fibonacci numbers
    if n <= 0:  # Base case for n = 0
        return 0
    elif n == 1:  # Base case for n = 1
        return 1
    else:
        ret                      ibonacci(n - 2)  # Sum of the two preceding numbers

n = 5  # Set the value of n
print(f"The {n}th Fibonacci number is: {fibonacci(n)}")  # Print the result

The 5th Fibonacci number is: 5
```

3.7
Arrays in Python

In Python, arrays are used to store collections of items, but unlike lists, all elements in an array must be of the same data type. While Python lists can accommodate values of varying types, arrays offer a more efficient way to manage data when uniformity is required. Since arrays are not a built-in data type in Python, you need to import the standard `array` module to work with them. You can do this using the following import statement:

> # import array

- Uniform Data Type: All elements within the array must be of the same type (e.g., all integers, all floats).
- Efficiency: Arrays offer more efficient memory usage compared to lists when working with large collections of data of the same type.
- Module Requirement: Arrays are not a built-in data type in Python, so you need to import them using the array module.

Syntax for Creating an Array:

> array_name = array.array(typecode, [initial_elements])

Q : Create a Python application that takes a user's input about their favorite book, including its title and a brief description. The application should perform the following tasks using string methods:

1. *Check if the book title is written in uppercase.*
2. *Find the maximum and minimum alphabetical characters in the book description.*
3. *Replace occurrences of the word "and" with "&" in the description.*

Step 1: Open Jupyter Notebook.

Step 2: Click on a new code cell to start typing.

Step 3: Rename the file (e.g., favorite_book_analysis.ipynb).

Step 4: Get input from the user for the book title and description.

book_title = input("Enter the title of your favorite book: ")

book_description = input("Enter a brief description of the book: ")

Step 5: Implement the following tasks:

- Check if the book title is in uppercase using the .isupper() method.
- Find the maximum and minimum alphabetical characters in the description using the max() and min() functions.
- Replace "and" with "&" in the description using the .replace() method.

print("Is the book title in uppercase?", book_title.isupper()) # Check if the title is in uppercase

max_char = max(book_description) # Find the maximum character in the description

min_char = min(book_description) # Find the minimum character in the description

print("Maximum character in the description:", max_char) # Print maximum character

print("Minimum character in the description:", min_char) # Print minimum character

modified_description = book_description.replace("and", "&")

print("Modified description:", modified_description)

Step 6: Run the code and observe the results.

Output:

```
book_title = input("Enter the title of your favorite book: ")  # Get book title from the user

book_description = input("Enter a brief description of the book: ")  # Get book description from the user

print("Is the book title in uppercase?", book_title.isupper())  # Check if the title is in uppercase

max_char = max(book_description)  # Find the maximum character in the description
min_char = min(book_description)  # Find the minimum character in the description
print("Maximum character in the description:", max_char)  # Print maximum character
print("Minimum character in the description:", min_char)  # Print minimum character

modified_description = book_description.replace("and", "&")  # Replace 'and' with '&'
print("Modified description:", modified_description)  # Print modified description


Enter the title of your favorite book: Alchemist
Enter a brief description of the book: It is a Self-Help Book.
Is the book title in uppercase? False
Maximum character in the description: t
Minimum character in the description:
Modified description: It is a Self-Help Book.
```

3.8 Search Algorithms in Python

3.8.1 Sequential Search

Sequential search, also known as linear search, is an algorithm used to locate a specific value in a list by checking each element in order. This method continues until the desired element is found or the end of the list is reached. It is simple and effective but can be inefficient for large lists since it does not require the list to be ordered.

- **Works on Unsorted Lists**: No need for the list to be ordered.
- **Time Complexity**: O(n), where n is the number of elements in the list, because every element might need to be checked in the worst case.

3.8.2 Binary Search

Binary search is a highly efficient algorithm for finding a target value in a sorted array. It works by repeatedly dividing the search interval in half, eliminating the half that cannot contain the target value. This method is classified as a divide-and-conquer algorithm and operates in logarithmic time, making it significantly faster than sequential search for large datasets.

- **Requires Sorted Lists**: Can only be used on a sorted list.
- **Time Complexity**: O(log n), where n is the number of elements in the list, because the search space is halved with each step.

Q : Create a Python application that manages a hotel booking system. The application should allow users to input information about different rooms available in the hotel, including room numbers, types, and prices. It should perform the following tasks using arrays (lists):

1. *Add new room details.*
2. *Display all available rooms.*
3. *Search for a room by its number and display its details.*

Step 1: Open Jupyter Notebook.

Step 2: Click on a new code cell to start typing.

Step 3: Rename the file (e.g., hotel_booking_system.ipynb).

Step 4: Initialize arrays (lists) for storing room details.

rooms = []

Step 5: Implement functions to add rooms, display rooms, and search for a room.

def add_room(room_number, room_type, price): # Function to add a new room

room_details = {'room_number': room_number, 'room_type': room_type, 'price': price} # Create a dictionary for room details

rooms.append(room_details) # Add room details to the list

def display_rooms(): # Function to display all available rooms

if not rooms: # Check if there are no rooms available

print("No rooms available.")

return

print("Available Rooms:") # Print header

for room in rooms: # Iterate through each room

print(f"Room Number: {room['room_number']}, Type: {room['room_type']}, Price: ${room['price']}") # Display room details

def search_room(room_number): # Function to search for a room by its number

for room in rooms: # Iterate through each room

if room['room_number'] == room_number: # Check if room number matches

print(f"Room Number: {room['room_number']}, Type: {room['room_type']}, Price: ${room['price']}") # Display room details

return

print("Room not found.") # Print if room is not found

Step 6: Use a menu-driven approach to allow users to choose different options.

while True: # Infinite loop

print("\nHotel Booking System") # Print menu title

print("1. Add Room") # Menu option 1

print("2. Display Rooms") # Menu option 2

```
#    print("3. Search Room")  # Menu option 3

#    print("4. Exit")  # Menu option 4

#    choice = input("Enter your choice (1-4): ")  # Get user choice


#    if choice == '1':  # If user chooses to add room

#       room_number = input("Enter room number: ")  # Get room number

#       room_type = input("Enter room type: ")  # Get room type

#       price = float(input("Enter room price: "))  # Get room price

#       add_room(room_number, room_type, price)  # Call function to add room

#       print("Room added successfully.")  # Success message


#    elif choice == '2':  # If user chooses to display rooms

#       display_rooms()  # Call function to display rooms


#    elif choice == '3':  # If user chooses to search room

#       room_number = input("Enter room number to search: ")  # Get room number to search

#       search_room(room_number)  # Call function to search room


#    elif choice == '4':  # If user chooses to exit

#       print("Thank you for using the Hotel Booking System.")  # Exit message

#       break  # Exit loop


#    else:  # If user enters an invalid choice

#       print("Invalid choice. Please try again.")  # Error message
```

Step 7: Run the code to observe results.

Output :

```
Hotel Booking System
1. Add Room
2. Display Rooms
3. Search Room
4. Exit
Enter your choice (1-4): 1
Enter room number: 23
Enter room type: 2 BHK
Enter room price: 30
Room added successfully.
```

```
Hotel Booking System
1. Add Room
2. Display Rooms
3. Search Room
4. Exit
Enter your choice (1-4): 2
Available Rooms:
Room Number: 23, Type: 2 BHK, Price: $30.0
```

```
Hotel Booking System
1. Add Room
2. Display Rooms
3. Search Room
4. Exit
Enter your choice (1-4): 3
Enter room number to search: 23
Room Number: 23, Type: 2 BHK, Price: $30.0
```

```
Hotel Booking System
1. Add Room
2. Display Rooms
3. Search Room
4. Exit
Enter your choice (1-4): 4
Thank you for using the Hotel Booking System.
```

UNIT 4 - LISTS, TUPLES, DICTIONARIES

4.1 Lists

A list in Python is a versatile collection of values, where elements can be of any data type, arranged in a specific sequence. Lists are created by placing values separated by commas within square brackets [ ]. Each value in the list is referred to as an element or item. Lists in Python are dynamic, meaning they can grow and shrink in size. Additionally, lists can also contain other lists as elements, forming a nested list. This flexibility makes lists a powerful and commonly used data structure in Python.

Syntax for Creating a List:

> my_list = [1, 2, 3, 'apple', 4.5] # A list with different data types

Example of a Nested List:

> nested_list = [1, [2, 3], [4, 5, [6, 7]]] # A list containing other lists

Key Characteristics:

- **Indexing**: Elements in a list can be accessed using their index, starting from 0.
- **Mutable**: Lists can be modified after creation (e.g., adding, removing, or changing elements).
- **Ordered**: The order of elements in a list is maintained, allowing retrieval of items in a specific sequence.

Q : Write a program to create a list of fruits, a nested list of more fruits, and demonstrate how to access elements from both the simple and nested lists.

Step 1: Open Jupyter Notebook.

Step 2: Click on a new code cell to start typing.

Step 3: Rename the file (eg. *list_example.ipynb.*)

Step 4: In a new code cell, create a list with various data types (e.g., strings, integers, booleans) and a nested list.

fruits = ['apple', 'banana', 'cherry', 42, True]

nested_list = ['orange', 'grapes', ['strawberry', 'blueberry'], 'mango']

Step 5: Access elements from both the main list and the nested list.

Step 6: Print the lists and specific elements to check the output.

print("Main list:", fruits)

print("Nested list:", nested_list)

print("Access item from nested list:", nested_list[2][1])

Step 7: Run the code by pressing Shift + Enter or clicking the Run button.

Output :

```
M  fruits = ['apple', 'banana', 'cherry', 42, True]
   nested_list = ['orange', 'grapes', ['strawberry', 'blueberry'], 'mango']


   print("Main list:", fruits)
   print("Nested list:", nested_list)
   print("Access item from nested list:", nested_list[2][1])

   Main list: ['apple', 'banana', 'cherry', 42, True]
   Nested list: ['orange', 'grapes', ['strawberry', 'blueberry'], 'mango']
   Access item from nested list: blueberry
```

4.1.1 List slice

A list slice is a portion or subset of elements from a list extracted using the slicing operator [:]. The slice is defined by two indices, m, and n, and is represented as [m:n]. This returns a new list containing elements from index m (inclusive) to index n (exclusive). Slicing allows for selective extraction of parts of a list without modifying the original list.

- If the first index m is omitted, the slice starts from the beginning of the list.
- If the second index n is omitted, the slice continues to the end of the list.
- If m >= n, the slice returns an empty list.
- If both indices are omitted, the entire list is returned.

Q: Imagine you have a list of carbon footprint activities for a week (activities = ["Travel", "Energy", "Water", "Waste", "Food"]). You want to extract just the middle activities for the three days. How would you use list slicing to achieve this?

Step 1: Open Jupyter Notebook.

Step 2: Click on a new code cell to start typing.

Step 3: Rename the file (e.g., List_Slicing_Example.ipynb)**.**

Step 4: Define a list with activities.

activities = ["Travel", "Energy", "Water", "Waste", "Food"]

Step 5: Use slicing to extract the middle activities.

middle_activities = activities[1:4]

Step 6: Print the sliced list.

print(middle_activities)

Step 7: Run the code by pressing Shift + Enter or clicking the Run button.

Output:

```
▶ # Define the list of carbon footprint activities
  activities = ["Travel", "Energy", "Water", "Waste", "Food"]

  # Use list slicing to get activities from index 1 to 4 (inclusive of 1, exclusive of 4)
  middle_activities = activities[1:4]

  # Print the result
  print(middle_activities)


  ['Energy', 'Water', 'Waste']
```

4.1.2 List Methods

Python provides several built-in methods for manipulating lists, allowing for operations like adding, removing, and sorting elements. These methods make it easy to manage and modify list data efficiently. Examples include append() to add an element, remove() to delete an element, and sort() to arrange elements in ascending order.

Method	Description	Example	Output
append(x)	Adds an element x to the end of the list	my_list.append(4)	[1, 2, 3, 4]
extend(iter)	Adds all elements of the iterable to the list	my_list.extend([4, 5])	[1, 2, 3, 4, 5]
insert(i, x)	Inserts an element x at index i	my_list.insert(2, 3)	[1, 2, 3, 4]
remove(x)	Removes the first occurrence of x from the list	my_list.remove(2)	[1, 3, 2]
pop([i])	Removes and returns the element at index i (last if not specified)	my_list.pop()	[1, 2], Returns: 3
clear()	Removes all elements from the list	my_list.clear()	[]
index(x)	Returns the index of the first occurrence of x	my_list.index(2)	1
count(x)	Returns the number of occurrences of x	my_list.count(2)	2
sort()	Sorts the list in ascending order	my_list.sort()	[1, 2, 3]
reverse()	Reverses the order of elements in the list	my_list.reverse()	[3, 2, 1]

copy()	Returns a shallow copy of the list	copied_list = my_list.copy()	copied_list = [1, 2, 3]

Q: You have a list of books in your reading list (books = ["The Great Gatsby", "1984", "To Kill a Mockingbird", "Pride and Prejudice", "Moby Dick"]). How can you manipulate this list using various list methods?

Step 1: Open Jupyter Notebook.

Step 2: Click on a new code cell to start typing.

Step 3: Rename the file (e.g., List_Methods_Books_Example.ipynb).

Step 4: Define a list with books.

books = ["The Great Gatsby", "1984", "To Kill a Mockingbird", "Pride and Prejudice", "Moby Dick"]

Step 5: Use the append method to add a new book to the list.

books.append("Brave New World")

Step 6: Use the count method to find how many times "1984" appears in the list.

book_count = books.count("1984")

Step 7: Use the extend method to add multiple books at once.

books.extend(["The Catcher in the Rye", "Fahrenheit 451"])

Step 8: Use the index method to find the index of "Pride and Prejudice".

pride_index = books.index("Pride and Prejudice")

Step 9: Use the pop method to remove the last book from the list.

removed_book = books.pop()

Step 10: Print the results

print("Updated Books List:", books)

print("Count of '1984':", book_count)

print("Index of 'Pride and Prejudice':", pride_index)

print("Removed Book:", removed_book)

Step 11: Run the code by pressing Shift + Enter or clicking the Run button.

Output:

```
▶ # Define the list of books
  books = ["The Great Gatsby", "1984", "To Kill a Mockingbird", "Pride and Prejudice", "Moby Dick"]

  # Use the append method to add a new book
  books.append("Brave New World")

  # Use the count method to find how many times "1984" appears
  book_count = books.count("1984")

  # Use the extend method to add multiple books at once
  books.extend(["The Catcher in the Rye", "Fahrenheit 451"])

  # Use the index method to find the index of "Pride and Prejudice"
  pride_index = books.index("Pride and Prejudice")

  # Use the pop method to remove the last book
  removed_book = books.pop()

  # Print results
  print("Updated Books List:", books)
  print("Count of '1984':", book_count)
  print("Index of 'Pride and Prejudice':", pride_index)
  print("Removed Book:", removed_book)


  Updated Books List: ['The Great Gatsby', '1984', 'To Kill a Mockingbird', 'Pride and Prejudice', 'Moby Dick', 'Brave New Wor
  ld', 'The Catcher in the Rye']
  Count of '1984': 1
  Index of 'Pride and Prejudice': 3
  Removed Book: Fahrenheit 451
```

4.1.3 List Loop

A **list loop** refers to the process of iterating over the elements of a list to perform specific operations or to access each item in the list. This is commonly achieved using a for loop in Python, which allows you to execute a block of code for each item in the list. List loops are useful for tasks such as modifying list items, performing calculations, or simply printing the elements of the list.

Benefits:

- Allows easy access to each element in the list.
- Simplifies code by reducing the need for index management.
- Facilitates operations like modifying, calculating, or printing elements.
- Enhances readability and maintainability of the code.
- Efficiently handles repetitive tasks with minimal effort.

Q: You have a list of fruits (fruits = ["Apple", "Banana", "Cherry", "Date", "Elderberry"]). Write a program using a loop to print each fruit along with its position in the list?

Step 1: Open Jupyter Notebook.

Step 2: Click on a new code cell to start typing.

Step 3: Rename the file (e.g., List_Loop_Example.ipynb).

Step 4: Define a list with fruits.

fruits = ["Apple", "Banana", "Cherry", "Date", "Elderberry"]

Step 5: Use a for loop to iterate over the list and print each fruit with its index.

for index, fruit in enumerate(fruits):

print(f"Fruit {index + 1}: {fruit}")

Step 6: Run the code by pressing Shift + Enter or clicking the Run button.

Output :

```
# Define the list of fruits
fruits = ["Apple", "Banana", "Cherry", "Date", "Elderberry"]

# Use a for loop to iterate over the list and print each fruit with its index
for index, fruit in enumerate(fruits):
    print(f"Fruit {index + 1}: {fruit}")


Fruit 1: Apple
Fruit 2: Banana
Fruit 3: Cherry
Fruit 4: Date
Fruit 5: Elderberry
```

4.1.4 List Parameters

When a list is passed as a parameter to a function in Python, the function receives a reference to the original list, not a copy. This means that any changes made to the list within the function will also be reflected in the original list outside the function. Lists are mutable, which allows them to be modified (like adding, removing, or updating elements) when passed to a function.

Q: Write a Python program that defines a list of numbers and a function my_insert() that inserts a new number at a specified index in the list. Show how passing the list as a parameter allows the function to modify the original list.

Step 1: Open Jupyter Notebook.

Step 2: Click on a new code cell to start typing.

Step 3: Rename the file (e.g., List_Parameters_Example.ipynb).

Step 4: Define a list of numbers (numlist).

numlist = [10, 20, 30, 40, 50]

Step 5: Define the function my_insert() to insert a value at a specific index in the list.

def my_insert(t, index, value):

t.insert(index, value)

Step 6: Call the function to insert 25 at index 2 in the list.

my_insert(numlist, 2, 25)

Step 7: Print the modified list to see the changes.

print(numlist)

Step 8: Run the code by pressing Shift + Enter or clicking the Run button.

Output:

```
▶ # Define the list of numbers
  numlist = [10, 20, 30, 40, 50]

  # Define a function to insert a value at a specific index in the list
  def my_insert(t, index, value):
      t.insert(index, value)

  # Call the function to insert 25 at index 2
  my_insert(numlist, 2, 25)

  # Print the modified list
  print(numlist)


  [10, 20, 25, 30, 40, 50]
```

4.1.5 Deleting list elements

The del statement in Python is used to delete elements from a list by specifying their index. When you use del, you can remove a single item or even an entire slice of the list, effectively modifying the original list. This operation does not return any value and directly affects the list, reducing its length accordingly.

For example:

del my_list[2] removes the element at index 2, while del my_list[1:3] removes the elements from index 1 to 2. Using del helps manage memory by freeing up space occupied by the deleted items.

Q: Write a Python program to remove the city "Chennai" from the list of cities (cities = ["Delhi", "Mumbai", "Chennai", "Bangalore", "Kolkata"]) using its index.

Step 1: Open Jupyter Notebook.

Step 2: Click on a new code cell to start typing.

Step 3: Rename the file (e.g., Remove_City_By_Index.ipynb).

Step 4: Define the list of cities.

cities = ["Delhi", "Mumbai", "Chennai", "Bangalore", "Kolkata"]

Step 5: Use the del operator to remove "Chennai" by its index (2).

del cities[2]

Step 6: Print the updated list to confirm the deletion.

print(cities)

Step 7: Run the code by pressing Shift + Enter or clicking the Run button.

```
▶  # Define the list of cities
   cities = ["Delhi", "Mumbai", "Chennai", "Bangalore", "Kolkata"]

   # Use the del operator to delete the element at index 2 (Chennai)
   del cities[2]

   # Print the updated list
   print(cities)


   ['Delhi', 'Mumbai', 'Bangalore', 'Kolkata']
```

4.1.6 Deleting List Elements

In Python, you can delete an element from a list using the del operator if you know the element's index. The del operator removes the element at the specified index, and the list is adjusted so that the elements that follow are shifted one position to the left. The del operator can also be used to delete slices of a list or even the entire list.

Syntax for deleting list elements using the del statement in Python

- ***Deleting a single element by index:***

        del my_list[index]

- ***Deleting a slice of elements:***

        del my_list[start_index:end_index]

- ***Deleting the entire list:***

        del my_list

Q: Write a Python program to remove the city "Chennai" from the list of cities (cities = ["Delhi", "Mumbai", "Chennai", "Bangalore", "Kolkata"]) using its index.

Step 1: Open Jupyter Notebook.

Step 2: Click on a new code cell to start typing.

Step 3: Rename the file (e.g., Delete_List_Elements.ipynb).

Step 4: Define the list of cities.

cities = ["Delhi", "Mumbai", "Chennai", "Bangalore", "Kolkata"]

Step 5: Use the del operator to remove "Chennai" by its index (2).

del cities[2]

Step 6: Print the updated list to confirm the deletion.

print(cities)

Step 7: Run the code by pressing Shift + Enter or clicking the Run button.

Output :

```python
▶ # Define the list of cities
  cities = ["Delhi", "Mumbai", "Chennai", "Bangalore", "Kolkata"]

  # Use the del operator to delete the element at index 2 (Chennai)
  del cities[2]

  # Print the updated list
  print(cities)


  ['Delhi', 'Mumbai', 'Bangalore', 'Kolkata']
```

4.1.7 Python Functions for List Operations:

Python provides several built-in functions and methods specifically designed for list operations. These functions make it easy to manipulate and interact with lists efficiently. Here's an overview of some commonly used functions for list operations:

- **cmp():** Compares two lists element by element (not available in Python 3.x).
- **len():** Returns the number of elements in a list.
- **max():** Returns the largest element in the list.
- **min():** Returns the smallest element in the list.
- **list():** Converts an iterable (like a tuple or string) into a list.

Function	Description	Syntax	Example	Output
cmp()	Compares two lists element by element (not available in Python 3.x).	cmp(list1, list2)	cmp([1, 2, 3], [1, 2, 3])	0 (equal)
len()	Returns the number of elements in a list.	len(list)	len([1, 2, 3])	3
max()	Returns the largest element in the list.	max(list)	max([1, 2, 3])	3
min()	Returns the smallest element in the list.	min(list)	min([1, 2, 3])	1
list()	Converts an iterable (like a tuple or string) into a list.	list(iterable)	list((1, 2, 3))	[1, 2, 3]

Q: Write a Python program to manage a list of product prices for an online store, using len(), max(), min(), and list() functions. Demonstrate these functions with practical operations such as counting the number of products, finding the highest and lowest prices, and converting a tuple of prices to a list. (Since cmp() is not available in Python 3, it is excluded from this example.)

Step 1: Open Jupyter Notebook.

Step 2: Click on a new code cell to start typing.

Step 3: Rename the file (e.g., List_Operations_Online_Store.ipynb).

Step 4: Define a tuple of product prices (product_prices_tuple).

product_prices_tuple = (299.99, 499.99, 199.99, 799.99, 649.99)

Step 5: Use the list() function to convert the tuple into a list.

product_prices = list(product_prices_tuple)

Step 6: Use the len() function to find the number of products.

num_products = len(product_prices)

Step 7: Use the max() function to find the highest product price.

highest_price = max(product_prices)

Step 8: Use the min() function to find the lowest product price.

lowest_price = min(product_prices)

Step 9: Print the results, showing the number of products, highest price, and lowest price.

print(f"Number of products: {num_products}")

print(f"Highest price: {highest_price}")

print(f"Lowest price: {lowest_price}")

Step 10: Run the code by pressing Shift + Enter or clicking the Run button.

Output:

```
 ▶ # Define a tuple of product prices
   product_prices_tuple = (299.99, 499.99, 199.99, 799.99, 649.99)

   # Convert the tuple to a list
   product_prices = list(product_prices_tuple)

   # Find the number of products
   num_products = len(product_prices)

   # Find the highest price
   highest_price = max(product_prices)

   # Find the lowest price
   lowest_price = min(product_prices)

   # Print the results
   print(f"Number of products: {num_products}")
   print(f"Highest price: {highest_price}")
   print(f"Lowest price: {lowest_price}")


   Number of products: 5
   Highest price: 799.99
   Lowest price: 199.99
```

4.1.8 List Comprehension

List comprehension is a concise and efficient way to create lists in Python. It allows you to generate a new list by performing an operation on each element of an existing sequence (like a list, tuple, or string), using a single line of code. List comprehension can also include conditions, making it a powerful tool for filtering and transforming data.

The general syntax of list comprehension is:

[expression for item in iterable if condition]

A list comprehension consists of the following parts:

- An Input Sequence.
- Variable representing members of the input sequence.
- An Optional Predicate expression.
- An Output Expression producing elements of the output list from members of the Input Sequence that satisfy the predicate.

Q: Write a Python program that generates a list of squares for all even numbers from an existing list of product quantities. Use list comprehension to create the list.

Step 1: Open Jupyter Notebook.

Step 2: Click on a new code cell to start typing.

Step 3: Rename the file (e.g., List_Comprehension_Example.ipynb).

Step 4: Define a list of product quantities.

quantities = [10, 15, 20, 25, 30, 35, 40]

Step 5: Use list comprehension to create a list of squares of even quantities.

squares_of_even_quantities = [q ** 2 for q in quantities if q % 2 == 0]

Step 6: Print the new list.

print(squares_of_even_quantities)

Step 7: Run the code by pressing Shift + Enter or clicking the Run button.

Output :

```
▶  # Define a list of product quantities
   quantities = [10, 15, 20, 25, 30, 35, 40]

   # Use list comprehension to generate squares of even quantities
   squares_of_even_quantities = [q ** 2 for q in quantities if q % 2 == 0]

   # Print the new list of squares
   print(squares_of_even_quantities)

   [100, 400, 900, 1600]
```

4.2 Tuples

A tuple is an ordered collection of values, which can be of different types. Like lists, tuples are indexed by integers, but unlike lists, tuples are immutable—meaning their elements cannot be changed after they are created. Tuples are useful when you want to store a collection of data that should not be modified.

Syntax for Creating a tuple:

    tuple_name = (value1, value2, value3)

Characteristics of Tuples:

- **Immutable:** Once a tuple is created, its elements cannot be changed, added, or removed.
- **Ordered:** Tuples maintain the order of elements, meaning that the position of items is preserved.
- **Heterogeneous:** Tuples can store elements of different data types, such as integers, strings, and other objects.
- **Hashable:** Since tuples are immutable, they can be used as keys in dictionaries, unlike lists.

Q: Write a Python program to create, update (by converting to a list), and delete a tuple of grocery items and their quantities in a grocery store inventory.

Step 1: Open Jupyter Notebook.

Step 2: Click on a new code cell to start typing.

Step 3: Rename the file (e.g., Tuple_Operations_Grocery.ipynb).

Step 4: Create a tuple with grocery items and their quantities.

groceries = ("Apples", 10, "Bananas", 20, "Milk", 5, "Bread", 3)

Step 5: Convert the tuple to a list to update the quantity of "Bananas."

grocery_list = list(groceries)

grocery_list[3] = 25 # Update "Bananas" quantity to 25

Step 6: Convert the list back to a tuple after the update.

groceries = tuple(grocery_list)

Step 7: Delete the entire tuple using del.

del groceries

Step 8: Print the updated tuple before deletion and confirm deletion.

print("Updated groceries:", groceries)

try:

print(groceries)

except NameError:

print("Tuple has been deleted.")

Step 9: Run the code by pressing Shift + Enter or clicking the Run button.

Output:

```python
# Step 4: Create a tuple of grocery items and their quantities
groceries = ("Apples", 10, "Bananas", 20, "Milk", 5, "Bread", 3)

# Step 5: Convert the tuple to a list to update an item
grocery_list = list(groceries)

# Update the quantity of "Bananas" to 25
grocery_list[3] = 25

# Step 6: Convert the list back to a tuple
groceries = tuple(grocery_list)

# Step 7: Print the updated tuple
print("Updated groceries:", groceries)

# Step 8: Delete the entire tuple
del groceries

# Step 9: Confirm tuple deletion
try:
    print(groceries)
except NameError:
    print("Tuple has been deleted.")


Updated groceries: ('Apples', 10, 'Bananas', 25, 'Milk', 5, 'Bread', 3)
Tuple has been deleted.
```

4.2.1 Tuple Methods:

- **count():** This method returns the number of times a specified element appears in the tuple.

    Syntax: tuple.count(element)

- **index():** This method returns the index of the first occurrence of a specified element in the tuple.

    Syntax: tuple.index(element)

Method	Syntax	Example	Output
count()	tuple.count(value)	my_tuple = (1, 2, 2, 3) my_tuple.count(2)	2
index()	tuple.index(value)	my_tuple.index(2)	1
len()	len(tuple)	len(my_tuple)	4
max()	max(tuple)	max((1, 2, 3))	3
min()	min(tuple)	min((1, 2, 3))	1
tuple()	tuple(iterable)	tuple([1, 2, 3])	(1, 2, 3)

Q: Write a Python program that creates a tuple of product categories in an e-commerce store. Use the count() method to check how many times a specific category appears, and use the index() method to find the position of a category.

Step 1: Open Jupyter Notebook.

Step 2: Click on a new code cell to start typing.

Step 3: Rename the file (e.g., Tuple_Methods_Example.ipynb).

Step 4: Create a tuple with product categories.

categories = ("Electronics", "Clothing", "Books", "Electronics", "Toys", "Electronics")

Step 5: Use the count() method to find how many times "Electronics" appears.

electronics_count = categories.count("Electronics")

Step 6: Use the index() method to find the first occurrence of "Books."

books_index = categories.index("Books")

Step 7: Print the results of both the count() and index() methods.

print(f"'Electronics' appears {electronics_count} times in the tuple.")

print(f"The first occurrence of 'Books' is at index {books_index}.")

Step 8: Run the code by pressing Shift + Enter or clicking the Run button.

Output:

```
H  # Step 4: Create a tuple with product categories
   categories = ("Electronics", "Clothing", "Books", "Electronics", "Toys", "Electronics")

   # Step 5: Use count() to find how many times "Electronics" appears
   electronics_count = categories.count("Electronics")

   # Step 6: Use index() to find the first occurrence of "Books"
   books_index = categories.index("Books")

   # Step 7: Print the results
   print(f"'Electronics' appears {electronics_count} times in the tuple.")
   print(f"The first occurrence of 'Books' is at index {books_index}.")


   'Electronics' appears 3 times in the tuple.
   The first occurrence of 'Books' is at index 2.
```

4.2.2 Built-in Functions with Tuples

Tuples, like other sequences in Python, can be operated on by several built-in functions. These functions allow for various operations such as finding the maximum and minimum values, summing elements, and more. Below are some of the commonly used functions with tuples:

1. **all():** Returns True if all elements in the tuple are True (or the tuple is empty).
2. **any():** Returns True if at least one element in the tuple is True.
3. **enumerate():** Returns an enumerate object, which contains the index and value of each tuple element.
4. **len():** Returns the number of elements in the tuple.
5. **max():** Returns the maximum value from the tuple.
6. **min():** Returns the minimum value from the tuple.
7. **sorted():** Returns a sorted list from the elements of the tuple.
8. **sum():** Returns the sum of all elements in the tuple (if the elements are numeric).

Function	Syntax	Example	Output
all()	all(tuple)	all((1, 2, 3))	TRUE
any()	any(tuple)	any((0, 1, 2))	TRUE
enumerate()	enumerate(tuple)	list(enumerate(('a', 'b', 'c')))	[(0, 'a'), (1, 'b'), (2, 'c')]
len()	len(tuple)	len((1, 2, 3))	3
max()	max(tuple)	max((1, 5, 3))	5
min()	min(tuple)	min((1, 5, 3))	1
sorted()	sorted(tuple)	sorted((3, 1, 2))	[1, 2, 3]
sum()	sum(tuple)	sum((1, 2, 3))	6

Q: Write a Python program to demonstrate the use of various built-in functions with a tuple of numerical values representing the monthly expenses of an individual.

Step 1: Open Jupyter Notebook.

Step 2: Click on a new code cell to start typing.

Step 3: Rename the file (e.g., Tuple_Builtin_Functions.ipynb).

Step 4: Create a tuple of monthly expenses.

expenses = (2000, 1500, 3000, 2200, 5000, 1700, 2500)

Step 5: Use the all() function to check if all expenses are greater than zero.

print("All expenses are non-zero:", all(expenses))

Step 6: Use the any() function to check if any expense is above 4000.

print("Any expense above 4000:", any(expense > 4000 for expense in expenses))

Step 7: Use enumerate() to display the month number and corresponding expense.

for i, expense in enumerate(expenses, 1):

print(f"Month {i}: {expense}")

Step 8: Use len() to find the total number of months in the tuple.

print("Total number of months:", len(expenses))

Step 9: Use max() and min() to find the highest and lowest expenses.

print("Maximum expense:", max(expenses))

print("Minimum expense:", min(expenses))

Step 10: Use sorted() to display the expenses in increasing order.

print("Sorted expenses:", sorted(expenses))

Step 11: Use sum() to calculate the total of all expenses.

print("Total expenses:", sum(expenses))

Step 12: Run the code by pressing Shift + Enter or clicking the Run button.

Output:

```python
▶ # Step 4: Create a tuple of monthly expenses
  expenses = (2000, 1500, 3000, 2200, 5000, 1700, 2500)

  # Step 5: Use all() to check if all expenses are greater than zero
  print("All expenses are non-zero:", all(expenses))

  # Step 6: Use any() to check if any expense is above 4000
  print("Any expense above 4000:", any(expense > 4000 for expense in expenses))

  # Step 7: Use enumerate() to display month number and corresponding expense
  for i, expense in enumerate(expenses, 1):
      print(f"Month {i}: {expense}")

  # Step 8: Use len() to find the total number of months
  print("Total number of months:", len(expenses))

  # Step 9: Use max() and min() to find the highest and lowest expenses
  print("Maximum expense:", max(expenses))
  print("Minimum expense:", min(expenses))

  # Step 10: Use sorted() to display expenses in increasing order
  print("Sorted expenses:", sorted(expenses))

  # Step 11: Use sum() to calculate the total of all expenses
  print("Total expenses:", sum(expenses))


  All expenses are non-zero: True
  Any expense above 4000: True
  Month 1: 2000
  Month 2: 1500
  Month 3: 3000
  Month 4: 2200
  Month 5: 5000
  Month 6: 1700
  Month 7: 2500
  Total number of months: 7
  Maximum expense: 5000
  Minimum expense: 1500
  Sorted expenses: [1500, 1700, 2000, 2200, 2500, 3000, 5000]
  Total expenses: 17900
```

4.2.3 Variable-length Argument Tuples

In Python, functions can be defined to accept a variable number of arguments using the *args syntax. When you prefix a parameter with an asterisk (*), it allows the function to accept any number of positional arguments. These arguments are then collected into a tuple, which can be processed within the function. This feature is particularly useful when you don't know in advance how many arguments will be passed to the function.

- **Flexibility**: The use of *args allows you to create functions that can handle varying amounts of input, making them more flexible and reusable.
- **Tuple Behavior**: Inside the function, args behaves like a tuple, allowing you to utilize tuple methods such as len(), count(), or iteration.
- **Order of Parameters**: When defining functions with variable-length arguments, *args should be placed after any regular positional parameters in the function signature.

Q: Write a Python program where a function called print_expenses accepts a variable number of expenses for different months and prints each one in a formatted manner.

Step 1: Open Jupyter Notebook.

Step 2: Click on a new code cell to start typing.

Step 3: Rename the file (e.g., Variable_Argument_Tuples_Example.ipynb).

Step 4: Define the function print_expenses with *expenses to accept multiple expenses as arguments.

def print_expenses(*expenses):

for i, expense in enumerate(expenses, 1):

print(f"Month {i}: ₹{expense}")

Step 5: Call the function with varying numbers of monthly expenses.

print_expenses(1500, 2300, 3100)

print_expenses(4000, 1800)

Step 6: Run the code by pressing Shift + Enter or clicking the Run button.

Output:

```
# Step 4: Define the function that accepts a variable number of arguments
def print_expenses(*expenses):
    for i, expense in enumerate(expenses, 1):
        print(f"Month {i}: ₹{expense}")

# Step 5: Call the function with different numbers of arguments
print_expenses(1500, 2300, 3100)
print_expenses(4000, 1800)


Month 1: ₹1500
Month 2: ₹2300
Month 3: ₹3100
Month 1: ₹4000
Month 2: ₹1800
```

4.3 Dictionaries

A dictionary in Python is an unordered collection of key-value pairs. Unlike lists, where elements are accessed by their position or index, dictionary elements are accessed using keys. These keys can be strings, numbers, or even tuples, and are used to retrieve the associated value. Dictionaries are extremely useful for scenarios like phone books, login pages, or any kind of mapping between two related pieces of information.

Syntax:

    my_dict = { "name": "John", "age": 30, "city": "New York" }

Characteristics:

- **Key-Value Pairs:** Each element in a dictionary consists of a key and its associated value. The key must be an immutable type (like strings, numbers, or tuples), while values can be of any data type.

- **Accessing Values:** You can access a value in a dictionary using its key:

  print(my_dict["name"]) # Output: John

- **Mutable:** You can add, remove, or change the items in a dictionary

- **Unordered:** The items in a dictionary do not maintain any specific order, meaning that the order in which items are added is not guaranteed to be the same when accessed.

- **Nested Dictionaries:** You can create dictionaries that contain other dictionaries, allowing for complex data structures.

Q: Write a Python program to create a dictionary that stores student names as keys and their scores as values. Implement functionality to add a new student, update a score, and remove a student from the dictionary.

Step 1: Open Jupyter Notebook.

Step 2: Click on a new code cell to start typing.

Step 3: Rename the file (e.g., Student_Scores_Dictionary.ipynb).

Step 4: Define a dictionary called student_scores that holds student names and scores.

student_scores = {"Sneha": 85, "Neha": 92, "Rahul": 78}

Step 5: Add a new student to the dictionary.

student_scores["Ankit"] = 88

Step 6: Update the score of an existing student.

student_scores["Sneha"] = 90

Step 7: Remove a student from the dictionary.

del student_scores["Rahul"]

Step 8: Print the updated dictionary to verify the changes.

print(student_scores)

Step 9: Run the code by pressing Shift + Enter or clicking the Run button.

Output:

```
▶ # Step 4: Define the dictionary with student names as keys and scores as values
  student_scores = {"Sneha": 85, "Neha": 92, "Rahul": 78}

  # Step 5: Add a new student to the dictionary
  student_scores["Ankit"] = 88

  # Step 6: Update the score of an existing student
  student_scores["Sneha"] = 90

  # Step 7: Remove a student from the dictionary
  del student_scores["Rahul"]

  # Step 8: Print the updated dictionary to verify the changes
  print(student_scores)


  {'Sneha': 90, 'Neha': 92, 'Ankit': 88}
```

4.3.1 Built-in Dictionary Functions & Methods

Dictionaries in Python come with several built-in functions and methods that facilitate common operations, such as accessing, modifying, and managing dictionary data. Below is a table summarizing these methods, along with their descriptions and examples.

Method	Description	Example	Output
dict()	Creates a new dictionary.	new_dict = dict(name="Alice", age=25)	{'name': 'Alice', 'age': 25}
len()	Returns the number of key-value pairs in the dictionary.	len(student)	3
clear()	Removes all items from the dictionary.	student.clear()	{}
copy()	Returns a shallow copy of the dictionary.	copy_dict = student.copy()	{'name': 'Alice', 'age': 22, 'GPA': 3.9}
get(key)	Returns the value for the specified key; returns None if the key is not found.	student.get("age")	22
items()	Returns a view object containing key-value pairs as tuples.	student.items()	dict_items([('name', 'Alice'), ('age', 22), ('GPA', 3.9)])
keys()	Returns a view object containing all keys in the dictionary.	student.keys()	dict_keys(['name', 'age', 'GPA'])

pop(key)	Removes the specified key and returns its value.	student.pop("GPA")	3.9
popitem()	Removes and returns the last inserted key-value pair.	student.popitem()	('GPA', 3.9)
update(other_di ct)	Updates the dictionary with elements from another dictionary.	student.update({"major": "Biology"})	{'name': 'Alice', 'age': 22, 'GPA': 3.9, 'major': 'Biology'}
values()	Returns a view object containing all values in the dictionary.	student.values()	dict_values(['Alice', 22, 'Biology'])

Q: Write a Python program to manage a company's employee records, where you can perform tasks such as adding new employees, checking the number of employees, comparing two departments' records, clearing the records, and more using dictionary functions and methods.

Step 1: Open Jupyter Notebook.

Step 2: Click on a new code cell to start typing.

Step 3: Rename the file (e.g., Employee_Management_Dictionary.ipynb).

Step 4: Create two dictionaries, dept1 and dept2, to represent two different departments with employee names and their respective IDs.

dept1 = {"Amit": 101, "Neha": 102, "Sneha": 103}

dept2 = {"Rahul": 201, "Priya": 202}

Step 5: Use len() to find out the number of employees in dept1.

print("Number of employees in Dept 1:", len(dept1))

Step 6: Use sorted() to sort the keys (employee names) in dept1.

print("Sorted Dept 1 employees:", sorted(dept1))

Step 7: Use dict1.update(dict2) to merge both departments into dept1.

dept1.update(dept2)

Step 8: Use dept1.pop("Neha") to remove an employee by name.

dept1.pop("Neha")

Step 9: Use dept1.keys() and dept1.items() to retrieve all employee names and the complete list of employee records.

\# print("Employees in Dept 1:", dept1.keys())

\# print("Complete employee records:", dept1.items())

Step 10: Use dept1.clear() to clear all employee records.

\# dept1.clear()

Step 11: Run the code by pressing Shift + Enter or clicking the Run button.

Output:

```
# Step 4: Create two dictionaries for employee records in two departments
dept1 = {"Amit": 101, "Neha": 102, "Sneha": 103}
dept2 = {"Rahul": 201, "Priya": 202}

# Step 5: Use len() to find out the number of employees in dept1
print("Number of employees in Dept 1:", len(dept1))

# Step 6: Use sorted() to sort the keys (employee names) in dept1
print("Sorted Dept 1 employees:", sorted(dept1))

# Step 7: Use update() to merge dept2 into dept1
dept1.update(dept2)
print("Merged employee records:", dept1)

# Step 8: Use pop() to remove an employee by name
dept1.pop("Neha")
print("Dept 1 after removing Neha:", dept1)

# Step 9: Use keys() and items() to retrieve all employee names and complete records
print("Employees in Dept 1:", dept1.keys())
print("Complete employee records:", dept1.items())

# Step 10: Use clear() to clear all employee records
dept1.clear()
print("Dept 1 after clearing records:", dept1)


Number of employees in Dept 1: 3
Sorted Dept 1 employees: ['Amit', 'Neha', 'Sneha']
Merged employee records: {'Amit': 101, 'Neha': 102, 'Sneha': 103, 'Rahul': 201, 'Priya': 202}
Dept 1 after removing Neha: {'Amit': 101, 'Sneha': 103, 'Rahul': 201, 'Priya': 202}
Employees in Dept 1: dict_keys(['Amit', 'Sneha', 'Rahul', 'Priya'])
Complete employee records: dict_items([('Amit', 101), ('Sneha', 103), ('Rahul', 201), ('Priya', 202)])
Dept 1 after clearing records: {}
```

Q: Write a Python program to manage student grades in a class. Your program should allow you to access a student's grade, update an existing grade, add a new student with their grade, delete a student's record, sort the dictionary by student names, and iterate through the dictionary to display all students and their grades.

Step 1: Open Jupyter Notebook.

Step 2: Click on a new code cell to start typing.

Step 3: Rename the file (e.g., Student_Grades_Management.ipynb).

Step 4: Create a dictionary grades to store student names as keys and their grades as values.

\# grades = {"Amit": 85, "Neha": 92, "Sneha": 78, "Rahul": 88}

Step 5: Access Neha's grade by referencing her name as a key.

print("Neha's Grade:", grades["Neha"])

Step 6: Update Sneha's grade to 82.

grades["Sneha"] = 82

Step 7: Add a new student, Priya, with a grade of 90.

grades["Priya"] = 90

Step 8: Delete Amit's record using the del statement.

del grades["Amit"]

Step 9: Sort the dictionary by student names and display the sorted result.

sorted_grades = dict(sorted(grades.items()))

Step 10: Iterate through the dictionary and print each student's name and grade.

for student, grade in grades.items():

print(f"{student}: {grade}")

Step 11: Run the code by pressing Shift + Enter or clicking the Run button.

Output:

```python
# Step 4: Create a dictionary for student grades
grades = {"Amit": 85, "Neha": 92, "Sneha": 78, "Rahul": 88}

# Step 5: Access Neha's grade
print("Neha's Grade:", grades["Neha"])

# Step 6: Update Sneha's grade
grades["Sneha"] = 82
print("Updated Sneha's Grade:", grades["Sneha"])

# Step 7: Add a new student Priya with a grade of 90
grades["Priya"] = 90
print("Added Priya's Grade:", grades)

# Step 8: Delete Amit's record
del grades["Amit"]
print("Grades after removing Amit:", grades)

# Step 9: Sort the dictionary by student names
sorted_grades = dict(sorted(grades.items()))
print("Sorted Grades by Student Names:", sorted_grades)

# Step 10: Iterate through the dictionary to display all student grades
print("All Students and their Grades:")
for student, grade in grades.items():
    print(f"{student}: {grade}")


Neha's Grade: 92
Updated Sneha's Grade: 82
Added Priya's Grade: {'Amit': 85, 'Neha': 92, 'Sneha': 82, 'Rahul': 88, 'Priya': 90}
Grades after removing Amit: {'Neha': 92, 'Sneha': 82, 'Rahul': 88, 'Priya': 90}
Sorted Grades by Student Names: {'Neha': 92, 'Priya': 90, 'Rahul': 88, 'Sneha': 82}
All Students and their Grades:
Neha: 92
Sneha: 82
Rahul: 88
Priya: 90
```

UNIT 5 - FILES, MODULES, PACKAGES

5.1 Reading and Writing Files in Python

Python provides convenient built-in methods, read() and write(), to facilitate reading from and writing to files. These methods allow for efficient data manipulation within file objects, making file handling straightforward and effective.

5.1.1 The write() Method

The write() method is employed to write data to a file. When using this method, it's essential to understand that if the specified file already exists, the content of that file will be overwritten by default. To prevent overwriting and to add content to an existing file, the file should be opened in append mode using the 'a' mode.

Syntax:

    file.write(data)

5.1.2 The read() Method

The read() method is utilized to read data from a file. Depending on the argument provided, this method can read the entire file or specific portions of it. If no argument is given, read() reads until the end of the file.

Syntax:

    file.read(size)

The write() and read() methods are fundamental tools in Python for file manipulation. The write() method allows for creating and updating file content, while the read() method enables reading data, whether it's the entire file or a specific segment. Together, they form the basis for efficient file handling in Python.

Q: Write a Python program to store a grocery shopping list into a file, read the file's contents, and display it.

Step 1: Open Jupyter Notebook.

Step 2: Click on a new code cell to start typing.

Step 3: Rename the file (e.g., Grocery_List_File_Operations.ipynb).

Step 4: Open a new text file named grocery_list.txt in write mode ('w').

file = open("grocery_list.txt", "w")

Step 5: Write some items into the file (e.g., grocery shopping list).

file.write("1. Apples\n")

file.write("2. Bananas\n")

\# file.write("3. Milk\n")

\# file.write("4. Bread\n")

Step 6: Close the file after writing the data to ensure changes are saved.

\# file.close()

Step 7: Open the file again, but now in read mode ('r'), and read the content.

\# file = open("grocery_list.txt", "r")

\# data = file.read()

Step 8: Print the file's contents to display the shopping list.

\# print("Grocery List:\n", data)

Step 9: Close the file after reading.

\# file.close()

Step 10: Run the code by pressing Shift + Enter or clicking the Run button.

Output:

```python
# Step 4: Open the file in write mode
file = open("grocery_list.txt", "w")

# Step 5: Write grocery items to the file
file.write("1. Apples\n")
file.write("2. Bananas\n")
file.write("3. Milk\n")
file.write("4. Bread\n")

# Step 6: Close the file
file.close()

# Step 7: Open the file in read mode
file = open("grocery_list.txt", "r")

# Step 8: Read the contents of the file
data = file.read()

# Step 9: Print the file contents
print("Grocery List:\n", data)

# Step 9: Close the file
file.close()


Grocery List:
 1. Apples
2. Bananas
3. Milk
4. Bread
```

5.2 File Handling Functions in Python

Python provides several built-in functions for file handling that enable you to perform various operations on file objects. Here, we will explore functions such as fileno(), seek(), tell(), read(), and close() to demonstrate their usage.

Function	Syntax	Description	Example
fileno()	file_object.fileno()	Returns the file descriptor for the file	python with open('example.txt', 'w') as file: print("File Descriptor:", file.fileno())

		object.	
seek()	file_object.seek(offset, whence)	Changes the current position of the file pointer.	python with open('example.txt', 'r+') as file: file.seek(0) print("Current position after seek:", file.tell())
tell()	file_object.tell()	Returns the current position of the file pointer.	python with open('example.txt', 'r') as file: print("Current position:", file.tell()) file.read(5) print("Current position after reading 5 bytes:", file.tell())
read()	file_object.read(size)	Reads up to size bytes from the file.	python with open('example.txt', 'r') as file: content = file.read(10) print("Content read:", content)
close()	file_object.close()	Closes the file, freeing up system resources.	python file = open('example.txt', 'a') file.write("\nAdding another line.") file.close()

Q: Write a Python program to create a text file, write a few lines into it, read specific content, and use functions like fileno(), seek(), tell(), read(), and close() to demonstrate file handling in Python.

Step 1: Open Jupyter Notebook.

Step 2: Click on a new code cell to start typing.

Step 3: Rename the file (e.g., File_Functions_Demo.ipynb).

Step 4: Open a file named demo_file.txt in write mode and write a few lines into it.

file = open("demo_file.txt", "w")

file.writelines(["Hello World!\n", "Python is fun.\n", "Learning file handling.\n"])

Step 5: Close the file to save the changes.

file.close()

Step 6: Reopen the file in read mode ('r') and demonstrate the read() method to read a few characters.

file = open("demo_file.txt", "r")

print(file.read(12)) # Read the first 12 characters

Step 7: Use the tell() function to show the current position of the file pointer.

print("Current file pointer position:", file.tell())

Step 8: Use the seek() function to move the file pointer back to the beginning.

file.seek(0)

Step 9: Use readline() to read a single line from the file.

print("First line using readline():", file.readline())

Step 10: Use the fileno() function to print the file's descriptor number.

print("File descriptor number:", file.fileno())

Step 11: Close the file after all operations.

file.close()

Step 12: Run the code by pressing Shift + Enter or clicking the Run button.

Output:

```python
# Step 4: Open the file in write mode
file = open("demo_file.txt", "w")

# Write multiple lines to the file
file.writelines(["Hello World!\n", "Python is fun.\n", "Learning file handling.\n"])

# Step 5: Close the file
file.close()

# Step 6: Open the file in read mode
file = open("demo_file.txt", "r")

# Step 6: Read the first 12 characters
print(file.read(12))  # Output: Hello World!

# Step 7: Use the tell() function to get the current position of the file pointer
print("Current file pointer position:", file.tell())

# Step 8: Use seek() to reset the file pointer back to the start
file.seek(0)

# Step 9: Use readline() to read a single line
print("First line using readline():", file.readline())  # Output: Hello World!

# Step 10: Use fileno() to get the file descriptor
print("File descriptor number:", file.fileno())

# Step 11: Close the file
file.close()


Hello World!
Current file pointer position: 12
First line using readline(): Hello World!

File descriptor number: 3
```

5.3 Create, Rename, and Delete a file in Python

5.3.1 Creating a File

In Python, you can create a file by opening it in write mode ('w'). If the specified file does not exist, it will be created. If it does exist, the content will be overwritten.

Syntax:

    with open('filename.txt', 'w') as file:

5.3.2 Renaming a File

Renaming a file in Python can be done using the os module's rename() function. This function takes the current file name and the new file name as arguments, allowing you to change the name of an existing file.

Syntax:

os.rename('current_filename.txt', 'new_filename.txt')

5.3.3 Deleting a File

To delete a file in Python, you can use the os module's remove() function. This function will remove the specified file from the filesystem. If the file does not exist, an error will be raised.

Syntax:

os.remove('filename.txt')

Q: Write a Python program to create a file, rename it, and then delete the renamed file.

Step 1: Open Jupyter Notebook.

Step 2: Click on a new code cell to start typing.

Step 3: Rename the file (e.g., File_Renaming_Deleting.ipynb).

Step 4: Import the os module.

import os

Step 5: Create a new file named sample_file.txt and write some text into it.

with open("sample_file.txt", "w") as file:

file.write("This is a sample file.")

Step 6: Use the os.rename() method to rename the file to renamed_file.txt.

os.rename("sample_file.txt", "renamed_file.txt")

Step 7: Print a confirmation message that the file has been renamed.

print("File renamed to 'renamed_file.txt'")

Step 8: Use the os.remove() method to delete the renamed file.

os.remove("renamed_file.txt")

Step 9: Print a confirmation message that the file has been deleted.

print("File 'renamed_file.txt' deleted successfully.")

Step 10: Run the code by pressing Shift + Enter or clicking the Run button.

Output:

```
# Step 4: Import the os module
import os

# Step 5: Create a new file and write text into it
with open("sample_file.txt", "w") as file:
    file.write("This is a sample file.")

# Step 6: Rename the file
os.rename("sample_file.txt", "renamed_file.txt")

# Step 7: Print confirmation for renaming
print("File renamed to 'renamed_file.txt'")

# Step 8: Delete the renamed file
os.remove("renamed_file.txt")

# Step 9: Print confirmation for deletion
print("File 'renamed_file.txt' deleted successfully.")


File renamed to 'renamed_file.txt'
File 'renamed_file.txt' deleted successfully.
```

5.4 SyntaxError and Logical Error in Python

5.4.1 SyntaxError

A SyntaxError occurs when the code violates the grammatical rules of Python. This type of error prevents the code from running altogether.

SyntaxError: invalid syntax

5.4.2 Logical Error

A Logical Error occurs when the code runs successfully without any syntax errors, but it produces incorrect results or behaves unexpectedly. These errors are often harder to detect because the program does not crash; instead, it provides unintended output due to flawed logic in the code.

Q: Write a Python program that demonstrates both a SyntaxError and a Logical Error.

Step 1: Open Jupyter Notebook.

Step 2: Click on a new code cell to start typing.

Step 3: Rename the file (e.g., Syntax_Logical_Error_Demo.ipynb).

Step 4: Write a function that includes a syntax error.

def faulty_function():

print("This will cause a SyntaxError" # Missing closing parenthesis

Step 5: Write a function that contains a logical error.

def add_numbers(a, b):

return a - b # Logical error

Step 6: Call both functions.

faulty_function() # This will raise a SyntaxError

result = add_numbers(5, 3)

print("The sum is:", result) # This will show a Logical Error

Step 7: Run the code by pressing Shift + Enter or clicking the Run button.

Output:

```
# Step 4: Function with SyntaxError
def faulty_function():
    print("This will cause a SyntaxError"  # Missing closing parenthesis

# Step 5: Function with Logical Error
def add_numbers(a, b):
    return a - b  # Logical error: should be addition

# Step 6: Call both functions
# faulty_function()  # Uncommenting this will raise a SyntaxError
result = add_numbers(5, 3)
print("The sum is:", result)  # This will show a Logical Error


  Cell In[20], line 3
    print("This will cause a SyntaxError"  # Missing closing parenthesis

SyntaxError: '(' was never closed
```

5.5 Exceptions in Python

In Python, an exception is an event that occurs during the execution of a program that disrupts the normal flow of instructions. When an error occurs, Python raises an exception, which can be caught and handled using try and except blocks. Proper handling of exceptions allows programs to continue running or to exit gracefully, providing useful error messages.

Exception Type	Description	Example
ZeroDivisionError	Raised when attempting to divide by zero.	python try: result = 10 / 0 except ZeroDivisionError: print("Error: Division by zero is not allowed.")
ValueError	Raised when a function receives an argument of the right type but an inappropriate value.	python try: number = int("hello") except ValueError: print("Error: Invalid value for conversion to int.")
TypeError	Raised when an operation or function is applied to an object of inappropriate type.	python try: result = "Hello" + 5 except TypeError: print("Error: Cannot concatenate string and integer.")

IndexError	Raised when trying to access an element in a list using an index that is out of range.	python my_list = [1, 2, 3] try: print(my_list[5]) except IndexError: print("Error: Index out of range.")
FileNotFoundError	Raised when trying to open a file that does not exist.	python try: with open('non_existent_file.txt', 'r') as file: content = file.read() except FileNotFoundError: print("Error: The file does not exist.")

Q: Write a Python program that simulates a simple calculator. The program should attempt to divide two numbers and handle potential exceptions.

Step 1: Open Jupyter Notebook.

Step 2: Click on a new code cell to start typing.

Step 3: Rename the file (e.g., Simple_Calculator_With_Exceptions.ipynb).

Step 4: Define a function for division.

def divide_numbers(num1, num2):

return num1 / num2

Step 5: Write the main function to execute division with exception handling.

def main():

number1 = 10

number2 = 0 # This will cause a ZeroDivisionError

try:

result = divide_numbers(number1, number2)

print(f"The result of dividing {number1} by {number2} is: {result}")

except ZeroDivisionError:

print("Error: You cannot divide by zero!")

Step 6: Intentionally cause a ValueError.

invalid_number = "ten" # This is a string, should be an integer

try:

result = int(invalid_number)

print(f"The converted number is: {result}")

except ValueError:

print("Error: Invalid input! Cannot convert to an integer.")

Step 7: Call the main function.

main()

Step 8: Run the code by pressing Shift + Enter or clicking the Run button.

Output:

```python
# Step 1: Define a function for division
def divide_numbers(num1, num2):
    return num1 / num2

# Step 2: Main function to execute division with exception handling
def main():
    # Step 3: Define two numbers
    number1 = 10
    number2 = 0   # This will cause a ZeroDivisionError

    try:
        # Step 4: Attempt to divide the numbers
        result = divide_numbers(number1, number2)
        print(f"The result of dividing {number1} by {number2} is: {result}")
    except ZeroDivisionError:
        print("Error: You cannot divide by zero!")

    # Step 5: Intentionally cause a ValueError
    invalid_number = "ten"   # This is a string, should be an integer
    try:
        # Attempt to convert the invalid number to an integer
        result = int(invalid_number)
        print(f"The converted number is: {result}")
    except ValueError:
        print("Error: Invalid input! Cannot convert to an integer.")

# Step 6: Call the main function
main()


Error: You cannot divide by zero!
Error: Invalid input! Cannot convert to an integer.
```

5.6 Modules in Python

Modules in Python are files containing Python code that define functions, classes, and variables. They allow for the logical organization of Python code into manageable sections, promoting reusability and modular programming. By using modules, developers can avoid redundancy and make their code easier to read and maintain.

- Code reusability reduces redundancy and improves efficiency.
- Modules help organize code logically, making it easier to manage.
- They provide a namespace, preventing naming conflicts.
- Updating or fixing bugs in a module simplifies maintenance.
- Modules facilitate collaboration among developers.

- Access to Python's standard library offers ready-made solutions.
- Isolating functionality simplifies testing and debugging.

Q: *Write a Python program using the math module to calculate the area of a circle based on a given radius.*

Step 1: Open Jupyter Notebook.

Step 2: Click on a new code cell to start typing.

Step 3: Rename the file (e.g., Circle_Area_Calculation.ipynb).

Step 4: Import the math module.

import math

Step 5: Define a function to calculate the area of a circle.

def calculate_area(radius):

return math.pi * (radius ** 2)

Step 6: Write the main function to execute the area calculation.

def main():

radius = 5 # Example radius

area = calculate_area(radius)

print(f"The area of the circle with radius {radius} is: {area:.2f}")

Step 7: Call the main function.

main()

Step 8: Run the code by pressing Shift + Enter or clicking the Run button.

Output:

```python
# Step 1: Import the math module
import math

# Step 2: Define a function to calculate the area of a circle
def calculate_area(radius):
    return math.pi * (radius ** 2)

# Step 3: Main function to execute the area calculation
def main():
    # Step 4: Define the radius
    radius = 5  # Example radius
    # Step 5: Calculate the area
    area = calculate_area(radius)
    # Step 6: Print the result
    print(f"The area of the circle with radius {radius} is: {area:.2f}")

# Step 7: Call the main function
main()


The area of the circle with radius 5 is: 78.54
```

5.6.1 Writing modules

The **from ... import** * statement allows you to import all functions and variables defined in a module into your current namespace, while the **from ... import** statement allows you to import specific functions or variables from a module.

Creating and Using a Module :

Step 1: Open Jupyter Notebook.

Step 2: Click on a new code cell to start typing.

Step 3: Create a module file named support.py and define functions in it.

Create a module file named support.py

with open('support.py', 'w') as f:

f.write('''\

def add(a, b):

return a + b

def display(message):

print(message)

''')

Step 4: Run the code by pressing Shift + Enter or clicking the Run button.

Step 5: Create a new code cell to import the functions from the support module.

Import the functions from the support module

from support import add, display

Step 6: Define a main() function to utilize the imported functions.

def main():

result = add(10, 5) # Adding two numbers

display(f"The result of addition is: {result}")

Step 7: Call the main() function to execute the program.

Call the main function

main()

Step 8: Run the code by pressing Shift + Enter or clicking the Run button.

Output:

```
support  Last Checkpoint: 5 minutes ago   (autosaved)

View    Insert    Cell    Kernel    Widgets    Help

Run    Code
```

```python
# Create a module file named support.py
with open('support.py', 'w') as f:
    f.write('''\
def add(a, b):
    return a + b

def display(message):
    print(message)
''')
```

```python
# Importing specific functions from the support module
from support import add, display

# Main function to execute the program
def main():
    # Step 3: Use the add function
    result = add(10, 5)  # Adding two numbers
    # Step 4: Use the display function to show the result
    display(f"The result of addition is: {result}")

# Step 5: Call the main function
main()

The result of addition is: 15
```

5.7 PACKAGES

A **package** in Python is a way of organizing multiple related modules into a single directory hierarchy. This structure allows for better organization and modularity of code. Each package is represented as a directory that contains a special file called __init__.py, which may be empty but indicates to Python that the directory should be treated as a package. Packages can contain sub-packages and modules, enabling a hierarchical organization of code.

- Packages allow for better organization of related modules, making it easier to manage large codebases.
- They provide a hierarchical namespace, preventing naming conflicts between modules.

- Packages facilitate code reuse by allowing developers to distribute modules together as a single package.
- They enhance collaboration among teams by allowing modular development and easy sharing of code.
- Packages can be easily installed and managed using package management tools like pip.
- They promote a clean structure for projects, making it easier for developers to navigate and understand the code.
- Using packages helps streamline dependency management, ensuring that required modules are included together.

Q: Write a Python program to create a package named mypackage that contains two modules: module1.py with a function greet(name) that returns a greeting message, and module2.py with a function farewell(name) that returns a farewell message. Import these functions and display their outputs.

Step 1: Open Jupyter Notebook.

Step 2: Click on a new code cell to start typing.

Step 3: Create a package directory named mypackage and define two modules, module1.py and module2.py.

```python
# Create a package directory named mypackage

import os

# Create package directory and module files

os.makedirs('mypackage', exist_ok=True)

# Create module1.py

with open('mypackage/module1.py', 'w') as f:

f.write('''\

def greet(name):

return f"Hello, {name}!"

''')

# Create module2.py

# with open('mypackage/module2.py', 'w') as f:

# f.write('''\

# def farewell(name):

# return f"Goodbye, {name}!"

# ''')
```

Step 4: Run the code by pressing Shift + Enter or clicking the Run button.

Step 5: Create a new code cell to import the functions from the modules in mypackage.

from mypackage.module1 import greet

from mypackage.module2 import farewell

Step 6: Use the imported functions to greet and say farewell.

print(greet("Alice")) # Greeting

print(farewell("Alice")) # Farewell

Step 7: Run the code by pressing Shift + Enter or clicking the Run button.

OUTPUT:

```
# Import the functions from the modules in mypackage
from mypackage.module1 import greet
from mypackage.module2 import farewell

# Use the functions from the imported modules
print(greet("Alice"))    # Greeting
print(farewell("Alice"))  # Farewell


Hello, Alice!
Goodbye, Alice!
```